BATIK, TIE DYEING, STENCILING, SILK SCREEN, BLOCK PRINTING

THE HAND DECORATION OF FABRICS

BATIK, TIE DYEING, STENCILING, SILK SCREEN, BLOCK PRINTING

THE HAND DECORATION OF FABRICS

Francis J. Kafka

Professor of Education,
Millersville State College, Millersville,
Pennsylvania

DOVER PUBLICATIONS, INC.

NEW YORK

Published in Canada by General Publishing Company, Ltd., 30 Lesmill Road, Don Mills, Toronto, Ontario.
Published in the United Kingdom by Constable and Company, Ltd.

This Dover edition, first published in 1973, is an unabridged republication of the work originally published by McKnight and McKnight Publishing Company in 1959 under the title *The Hand Decoration of Fabrics*.

International Standard Book Number: 0-486-21401-X
Library of Congress Catalog Card Number: 73-80948

Manufactured in the United States of America
Dover Publications, Inc.
180 Varick Street
New York, N. Y. 10014

Introduction

In the rapidly growing field of arts and crafts, no area has received more attention than that dealing with the decoration applied to fabrics. Yet in no area is so little information available between the covers of *one* book. The artist, the home craftsman, the art student, and the home economics student must search far and wide for the information needed. Some of the arts are ancient and their techniques have not been adequately recorded. Others are hemmed-in and surrounded by a vocabulary and a trade language so dimensioned as to make it impossible for the beginner to enjoy the thrill of accomplishment.

This text endeavors to take the beginner through a dozen or more techniques of applying decoration to fabrics, with simple, step-by-step instructions and illustration. The emphasis throughout the book is on self-explanatory illustrations and simple written procedures. The reader will realize that he is being *shown*, rather than *told*, how to do it! Each chapter deals with another technique or a portion of a technique, and each new technique presents a *different* method of applying a design or pattern to a piece of cloth. As each method is introduced to the craftsman, a short, condensed historical background of that particular method is presented. Immediately following this is a "get right down to work" explanation of the method — presented in picture form, with as few words as necessary to describe the method.

The beginner, regardless of his previous background or talents, is taken on a journey into this fascinating field of fabric decoration. If the craftsman is more advanced, he will experience the satisfaction of having a reference manual at his disposal, as even he learns some new "tricks of the trade." Both the beginner and the advanced craftsman will be able to start experimentation in each of the varied areas of decoration as soon as the chapter has been read. In most cases, the materials and equipment are already at hand. In *no* instance does expensive or hard-to-find equipment have to be obtained. The craftsman is even free to start with almost any section of the book!

In no area of arts and crafts will the satisfaction of quick results be experienced more readily than in the area of fabric decoration.

FRANCIS J. KAFKA

Acknowledgements

The author wishes to acknowledge with sincere appreciation the efforts of the following industrial firms, organizations, and individuals who contributed so generously in the preparation of this book:

Allied Reproduction Associates; The American Crayon Co.; Ardlee Associates; Behr-Manning Co.; Binney & Smith, Inc.; Chicago Natural History Museum; Colonial Process Supply Co.; CVH Laboratories Co.; The Davis Press, Inc.; DonJer Products Co.; Floquil Products, Inc.; General Electric Co.; M. Grumbacher, Inc.; Higgins Ink Co., Inc.; Monroe Chemical Co.; The Naz Dar Co.; Park & Tilford; The Republic of Indonesia Information Office; Sanco Piece Dye Works, Inc.; Tri-Chem, Inc.; Vertipile, Inc.; F. Weber Co.; Westinghouse Electric Corp.

Vera Andrus, Supervisor of the Photographic Research Division of the Metropolitan Museum of Art, New York; John Kent Tilton, Director of the Scalamandre Museum of Textiles, New York; Calvin S. Hathaway, Director of the Museum for the Arts of Decoration of The Cooper Union for the Advancement of Science and Art, New York; E. Alice Mosher, Professor of Art, Skidmore College, Saratoga Springs, N. Y.; Carmella Nesi, Former Principal, Tetard Junior High School, New York; Agnes Dress, Instructor of Home Economics, The Tetard Junior High School, New York; Marian C. Beckmann, Leonia, New Jersey; Hazel K. Mowdy, Berwick, Penn.

My special thanks are extended to William M. Jordan, my close friend and associate, without whose friendship, inspiration, and unfailing assistance, this task might have been less pleasant than it was.

F. J. K.

Contents

1. History of Textile Decoration **1**
2. Hand Stenciling of Fabrics **8**
3. Hand Stenciling a Scarf **16**
4. A Stenciled Border Repeat **20**
5. Planning An Over-All Repeat **25**
6. Over-All Repeat Patterns Stenciled in Two Colors **33**

   The Art of Batik **41**

   A Batik Handkerchief **53**
9. Tie Dyeing **58**
10. Linoleum Block Printing **67**
11. Linoleum Block Printing in Several Colors **82**
12. Other Types of Block Printing **89**
13. Freehand Painting **94**
14. Silk Screen Printing **102**
15. Silk Screening Repeat Patterns **116**
16. Silk Screen in Several Colors **128**
17. Added Suggestions in Silk Screen **139**
18. Novelty Decorations **146**
19. Color and Color Mixing **161**
20. Home Dyeing **167**
21. Caring For Decorated Fabrics **175**
22. Sources of Supply **179**
23. A Gallery of Samples **180**

Index **195**

To
WILLIAM M. JORDAN
Most Gifted of My Friends

CHAPTER I

History of Textile Decoration

Textile decoration, for the purpose of this text, will be that branch of the creative arts which embraces *any* method of applying color or design to a woven fabric. Since the earliest periods in the development of man's craftsmanship, samples have been produced which indicate that man has *woven* designs and motifs into his fabrics. It is those methods apart from this technique of *weaving* a design that this text will cover. More precisely, the book includes the following areas of textile decoration:

Stenciling. The technique of applying dyes or pigments through a *cut-out design or pattern.*

Batik. A *resist dyeing process* in which the design is applied to the fabric with a material which will *resist* the action of a dye. After dyeing, the resist substance is removed.

Block Printing. The method employed when carved blocks of wood, or other substances, are charged with paints or dyes and then *imprinted onto the fabric.*

Tie Dyeing. A *resist method of dyeing,* in which the portions of the fabric which are *not to be colored* are tied tightly with twine or cord prior to immersion in the dye bath.

Freehand Painting. This method, as the name implies, is the technique in which paint is applied, *freehand, with a brush.*

Silk Screen Printing. This is also a *stencil-type technique,* in that a cut-out design or pattern is employed. It adds the benefit, however, of a method of holding together numerous portions of a pattern, which is always a problem in stencil printing.

Novelty Decoration. This area will include the application of *flock, raised decoration,* and various other techniques.

Early Origins

Like so many of the decorative arts, the varied processes associated with applying decoration to textiles (as opposed to *woven* decoration) seem to be lost in antiquity. There appears to be little doubt that these arts had their origin in China, India, or Egypt. But precisely where or when is not known.

It is interesting to note that even in Europe where the wood block was used for book illustration in the 15th century, it was not until the 17th century that this technique was used for decorating textiles. Block printing appeared early in the Orient, samples having been found in China and Japan dating from the 8th and 9th centuries. It is only supposed, of course, that these prints were used on cloth as well as on other objects.

Fig. 1. Block Print on Linen - Germany, 13th Century (Courtesy, Cooper Union Museum)

The early blocks used for printing were made of stone or wood. The designs were scraped or scratched onto a smooth surface which was in turn inked in some manner and an impression transferred by "stamping" onto the cloth. Fig. 1 illustrates a sample of an early block print used on textiles. As the art developed, special wooden blocks were prepared, using end grain of certain woods only. Sometimes pieces of copper and brass were inserted into the wood to give fine line details. In reality, the modern printing press for printing textiles utilizes this block printing technique. Metal rollers, engraved with the design, are inked and rolled across the material being printed, Fig. 2.

Fig. 2. Textile Printing Press (Courtesy, Sanco Piece Dye Works)

Batik

Various specialized techniques for decorating textiles were developed in different parts of the world; and in many localities, they are still practiced in the original manner. *Batik* is probably foremost among these special forms.

Batik is a resist dyeing process in which molten wax is applied to the fabric prior to dyeing, thus resisting the action of the dye in those areas. After dyeing, the wax is removed and other areas are waxed-in prior to a second dyeing. One color covering another creates an additional color and thus the process continues.

Batik originated in either China or India, possibly as long as 1200 years ago. It is practiced throughout Indonesia for the decoration of everyday clothing. The

Fig. 3. Batik on Cotton - Java, 19th Century (Courtesy, Cooper Union Museum)

Fig. 4. Tie Dye on Silk - Bali, 19th Century (Courtesy, Cooper Union Museum)

art depends upon highly developed methods of applying the wax and the use of dyes which can be used without boiling (or the wax would be disengaged). The patterns are almost always free-flowing and liquid in appearance, registering as it were, the very technique which is used to apply it, Fig. 3. Many modern dress prints, while decorated by machine, simulate the batik appearance.

Tie Dye

Tie dye is another of the specialized techniques developed for decorating woven materials. It is practiced chiefly in Central India and on the island of Bali. It undoubtedly originated in one of these places. This, too, is a resist dye technique, but the resist action is accomplished by tying various portions of the material very tightly with thread or rope prior to dyeing it. The designs are most frequently circular or zig-zag in nature — a result of the fabric being tied in little clusters. Unlike batik however, the material may be boiled in dye, hence a wider range and greater intensity of color is possible, Fig. 4.

5

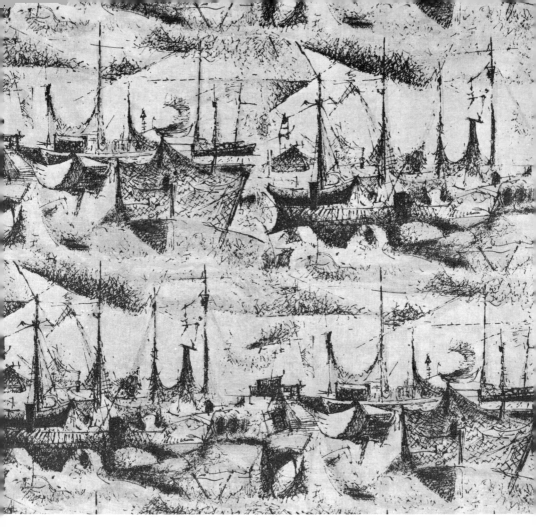

Fig. 5. Screen Print on Linen - "Tranquil Harbor" by Ezio Martinelli (Courtesy, Cooper Union Museum)

Stenciling

Stenciling is a technique which originated early in China and Japan and is probably one of the most widely used methods. In this process, a design is cut through a thin material, and paint or dye is then brushed through the open portions of the design. The Japanese developed stenciling to a high level of skill and eliminated bulky "ties" by using raw silk strands, and sometimes

6

hair, to hold the various portions of the design in place. The modern technique of silk screen printing is nothing more or less than an adaptation of the stencil technique. In silk screening, the stencil is attached to a thin mesh material, and the paint is forced through the mesh. The resulting imprint takes place only in those areas which are *open* in the stencil. A very large percentage of fine fabrics are printed by this method, Fig. 5.

The Ancient Arts

From all corners of the earth, man has contributed something of himself to the decoration of woven materials. Many of the arts have persisted only because one artisan was willing to teach another. Man's custom of recording the techniques and "secrets" of his art is a relatively new development compared to the ancient origins of some of these arts. Many of them, like batik and tie dye, are still practiced in certain areas in almost the original manner. Others, like block printing and stenciling, have given rise to machine printing and silk screen printing. The textile decorating industry is an important one in the world today. Yet man still decorates many of his fabrics by hand; hence, the arts really never die.

Additional References

Tilton, John Kent, *Two Hundred Years of Textile Designs*. New York: Scalamandre Museum of Textiles, n/d.

CHAPTER 2

Hand Stenciling of Fabrics

The stenciling technique is probably one of the oldest of all methods of decorating textile fabrics. In essence, it is what is generally known as a resist technique. In any *resist* technique, some device is employed which will prevent the paint or dye from penetrating certain areas. In the stencil technique this is done mechanically.

A design motif is cut out of a thin material, Fig. 6. This stencil is placed against the material to be decorated, and paint or dye is applied through it.

Fig. 6. Hand Stenciling

8

Those portions of the stencil plate which have been cut away, freely admit the paint, while those portions which remain solid *resist* the paint. Thus, the printed image is actually a *mechanically perfect* reproduction of the motif. Any originality in design must take place at the time the stencil plate is being cut. Beyond this point, at least theoretically, each print will look exactly like the one before it.

Limitations in Design

In this technique, however, the artist has always been restricted by the fact that certain *whole* areas cannot be cut out of the stencil without losing the full design. It will be noted that if the design in Fig. 6 were to contain a central design insert, Fig. 7, this insert would be *completely isolated* from the rest of the design. If the small insert design was first cut through the paper, Fig. 8, all would be well with the artist. When the large pattern were cut however, Fig. 9, the smaller design would be cut away with it. This restriction gave rise to the use of the "bridge" or "tie" which has identified the stencil design throughout history, Fig. 10.

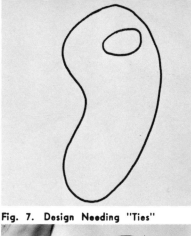

Fig. 7. Design Needing "Ties"

Fig. 8. Small Design Satisfactory

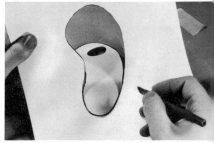

Fig. 9. Ties Are Needed

Fig. 10. Note Ties

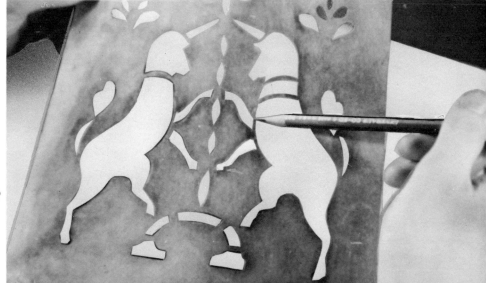

9

Fig. 11. Design Needing Ties

Fig. 12. Crude Ties

Fig. 13. More Graceful Ties

Fig. 14. Traditional Designs

It is important for the artist to remember this restriction when planning his pattern, because these ties or bridges must form as natural a part of the pattern as possible. If a concentric circular pattern is desired, for example, Fig. 11, the ties may be produced somewhat crudely as in Fig. 12. Or they can be gracefully blended into the basic shape as shown in Fig. 13. Some designs lend themselves more readily to this technique than others. It must also be kept in mind that since the stencil plate will have to be held flat against the printing surface while the paint is brushed over it, the design cannot be such that it will be impossible to keep all component parts of the plate flat against the printing surface. For this reason, most traditional stencil patterns have either consisted of a number of small open areas with many ties as component parts, or of large, single, open areas, Fig. 14.

Tools and Materials

All of the tools and materials needed are either available commercially or can be made or improvised. The commercial ones include the stencil cutting knife, waxed stencil board, stencil brushes, and special fabric paint, Fig. 15.

For the artist who wishes to improvise his equipment, an ordinary single-edge razor blade can be used for most cutting. For finer cutting, a small piece of razor blade can be carefully broken off with pliers and mounted in a wooden pen holder, Fig. 16. Many other kinds of craft knives, such as frisquet knives, silk screen stencil cutting knives, and whittling knives, can also be adapted for this purpose.

Fig. 15. Tools and Materials   Fig. 16. Improvised Cutter

Stencil board can be made by coating a good grade of bond paper with melted paraffin or shellac and allowing thorough drying before use. Discarded film negatives can also be used. While this material is more difficult to cut, it is also more durable. The discarded backing sheets from duplicating machine

Fig. 16a. Brushes (Courtesy, M. Grumbacher)   Fig. 17. Short Bristles

stencils, as well as printers' tympan paper, may also be used.

The decorations on textiles will need to be colorfast and washproof. A special liquid called a *mordant* can be mixed for a few cents. When used with ordinary printer's ink, this produces a colorfast and washproof fabric paint. To twelve parts of turpentine, add one part of acetic acid and about one-half part of oil of wintergreen. The term "part" can mean any standard quantity providing the same measure is used for all ingredients. Keep this mixture in a well-stoppered bottle marked, "Poison — Printer's Ink Mordant." To use, add this mordant to printer's ink until the mixture is of brushing consistency. A water soluble mordant can be made by straining the white of an egg through cheesecloth. To this, add about one teaspoon of vinegar. This mordant is added to tempera colors until brushing consistency is achieved.

Commercially available stencil brushes are inexpensive and can be obtained in a variety of sizes, Fig. 16a. However, any stiff-bristle brush may be used if the bristles are cut down so that most of the flexibility disappears from the brush, Fig. 17.

A small piece of glass is a good surface for mixing the paint or ink. The usual collection of pencils, thumb tacks, pressure adhesive tape, drawing paper,

12

tracing paper, etc., will all be used at some time. You will need a good supply of clean rags, old newspaper, and a cleaning solvent such as benzine or kerosene.

The Technique

1. Take any simple design which has been drawn or traced onto paper and fasten it on a piece of stiff cardboard, Fig. 18.

2. Place a piece of waxed stencil board over the design and fasten this in place; use pressure adhesive tape, Fig. 19. Waxed stencil board is sufficiently transparent that the design can be seen through it. If other kinds of stencil boards are used, the design should be transferred to the stencil material with carbon paper. From this point on, the steps will be the same.

3. Using either the stencil knife or a razor blade, cut the entire design through the stencil board — making clean, sharp cuts, Fig. 20. Where two cuts are to meet, extend each cut a trifle so that they cross,

Fig. 18. Fasten to Stiff Cardboard

Fig. 19. Stencil Board Over Design

Fig. 20. Make Clean, Sharp Cuts

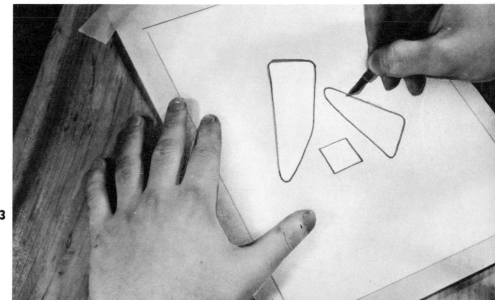

Fig. 21. Fasten the Stretched Cloth

Fig. 23. Work Paint into Brush

Fig. 24. Locate the Stencil

Fig. 25. Stroke To Open Area

Fig. 22. Mix Paint on Glass Square

rather than attempt to make a perfectly square cut at the corner. Fuzzy corners and edges will produce fuzzy lines in the finished print.

4. The cloth to be printed must be clean and free of starch and filler. It should be pressed flat. Either tack it to a wooden drawing board or pin it to a sheet of cardboard so that it is stretched and free from creases, Fig. 21.

5. Mix a small quantity of fabric paint on the square of glass, using a spatula or a splint of wood. Place this glass on several thicknesses of newspaper, Fig. 22.

6. Dip the stencil brush into the paint so that a very small quantity of the paint is taken up. Then work this quantity well into the brush on a clean area of the glass, Fig. 23.

7. Place the stencil in the proper location on the cloth, Fig. 24.

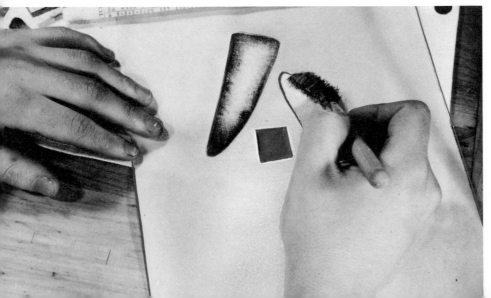

8. Apply paint to the cloth through the stencil by brushing firmly from *outside* the design outline *toward the open areas,* Fig. 25. Stroking in the opposite direction will force paint under the edges of the stencil and ruin the print.

9. The print is produced by *brushing the paint well into the fibers* of the material, and *not* by laying on a coating of paint. This is the reason for using a stiff brush. On most fabrics, the paint will penetrate through to the back. Two kinds of brush techniques are shown in Fig. 26. One is the solid area technique in which the paint is brushed in until the entire open area of the design is colored uniformly. The other technique (using the same stencil) is the shading technique. Here the paint is brushed toward the center, leaving irregular brush stroke marks and a color-free, highlighted area.

10. To clean the stencil, place it on a sheet of newspaper and wipe it clean with a rag moistened in solvent. Wipe in the same direction as the brush was applied, Fig. 27. Care should be taken that small bridges in the stencil are not damaged while cleaning. Brushes are cleaned thoroughly in solvent and then washed in soap and warm water.

11. After the print has air dried for twenty-four hours, heat-set it for three minutes with a moderately warm iron to assure color permanency, Fig. 28.

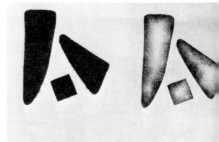

Fig. 26. Shaded and Solid Stenciling

Fig. 27. Clean Toward Open Areas

Fig. 28. Heat-Set for Permanency

CHAPTER 3

Hand Stenciling a Scarf

A scarf is an excellent object upon which the beginner can first try his hand at textile decorating. The stenciling technique is also a good starting activity because it is basic to so many of the other techniques.

Developing a Design

Before attempting to apply a decoration to a scarf, the artist should develop an original design. There are countless

Fig. 29. Make Free, Graceful "Scribbles"

16

books containing design motifs and hundreds of standard patterns which can be copied or traced. But should the individual who delights in hand decorating be content with a design which someone else has originated? Two basic types of design should interest the beginner: the freeform and the abstract.

The freeform design can be developed easily with either of two methods. It can be made by sketching a pleasing form, or with a scribbling technique. For the latter, take a large sheet of drawing paper; using a soft pencil, cover the sheet with a considerable amount of "scribbling," Fig. 29. When this scribbling is complete, examine the sheet carefully for several minutes until one or more shapes stand out as appealing. Color or fill-in these shapes completely, Fig. 30. Then cut them out and mount them on another sheet in a relationship which looks attractive and well-balanced (usually at least two of the shapes should touch each other), Fig. 31. The design is complete and ready to be cut into the stencil.

The abstract design is based on some natural form. Some artists trace outlines of shadows or light falling through a textured material. A common method is to start with a naturalistic form such as the flower in Fig. 32. Examine the form carefully and it will be noted that it contains certain basic shapes placed in relationship to each other. Place a sheet of tracing paper over the picture and with a pencil sketch in those basic shapes, Fig. 33. Remove the tracing paper, finish up the sketching, and an abstract design is ready for stencil cutting, Fig. 34.

17

Fig. 30. Fill In the Appealing Shapes

Fig. 31. Arrange in Pleasing Manner

Fig. 32. Start With Naturalistic Form

Fig. 33. Trace Basic Shapes

Fig. 34. Finished Abstract Design

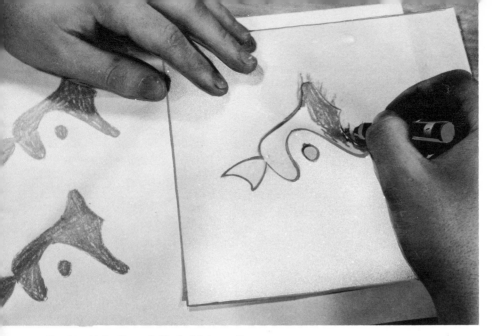

Fig. 35. Make Several Chalk Prints on Paper

Fig. 36. Arrange Prints

The Technique

1. Position and fasten the drawing under a piece of stencil board, and cut out the stencil as explained in the text accompanying Figs. 18, 19, & 20.

2. Using colored crayon or colored chalk, make as many prints of this stencil on drawing paper as it is planned to use on the finished product, Fig. 35.

3. Make sure that the scarf has been thoroughly washed and ironed flat. This is important even if the article is new.

4. Cut out the sample prints which were made on paper and place them on the scarf in different locations until the desired locations are determined, Fig. 36.

5. Place the stencil on top of each print. Using small pieces of pressure adhesive tape, mark the position of the upper right-hand corner

of the stencil in each location. This is known as *registering the stencil*, Fig. 37.

6. Remove the paper prints, and mix the paint on the glass slab. Proceed to apply the paint through the stencil, using the corner register marks to locate the stencil properly before each print, Fig. 38.

7. After the scarf has air dried for twenty-four hours, it should be heat set to insure permanency of the colors. When ironing a large article such as a scarf, a damp cloth should be placed over the scarf before applying the iron. A steam iron may be used instead. Fig. 39 shows the finished article.

Fig. 37. Make Register Marks

Cleaning Up

Brushes and stencils should be cleaned immediately after use. Most textile paint is designed to "set" completely in normal room air. It will set on the brush and the stencil as well, making it impossible to remove. The artist should also exercise great care to keep the work clean — this means the hands and any other equipment which is used. A small spot of paint accidentally applied to the fabric is generally impossible to remove.

Fig. 38. Stencil the Design

Fig. 39. Finished Scarf

Additional Project Suggestions

This variety of spot stencil design can be applied to:

Handkerchiefs
Face Towels
Kerchiefs
Napkins
Finger Towels
T-Shirts
Guest Towels
Shirt Pockets
Aprons

CHAPTER 4

A Stenciled Border Repeat

Fig. 40. Repeat Design on Curtain

In textile decoration the vast majority of the designs applied are printed in some pattern of repeat over the entire cloth or border of the cloth. In the previous experiments the spot design was printed several times in no special arrangement. In this chapter a design will be developed that can be repeated along the edge of window curtain material, Fig. 40.

Fig. 41. Cut Straight-Edged Pieces

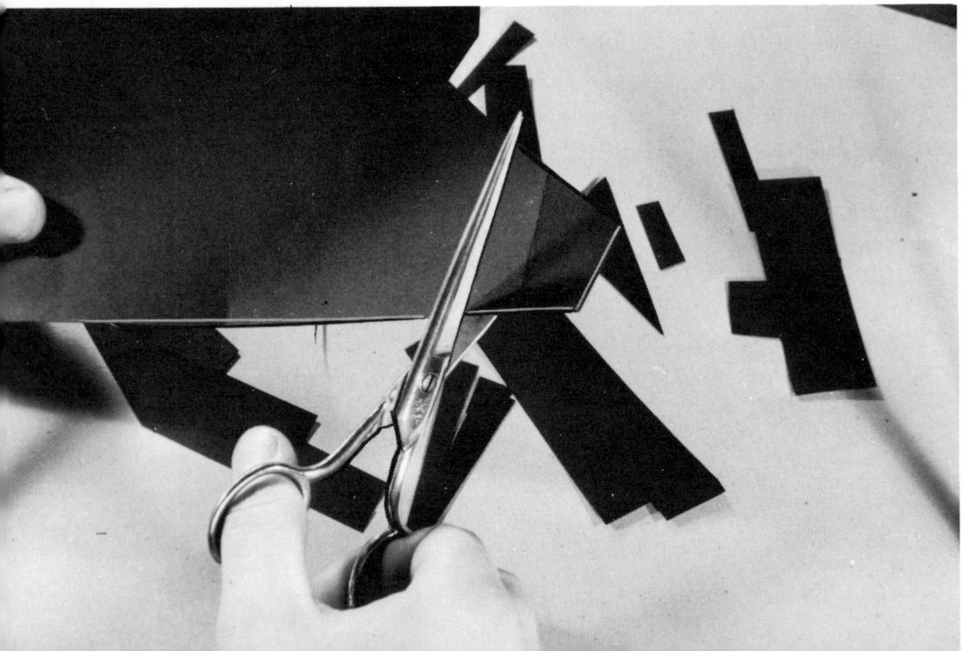

Fig. 42. Arrange Pieces

To develop an appropriate design, the "cut paper" method will be used. Using a sheet of black construction paper and scissors, cut about a dozen small pieces all having straight edges, Fig. 41. Depending upon the length of the border to be printed, decide upon the width of the pattern unit. (In the ilustration, the unit is approximately eight inches long.) Take a number of the pieces of cut paper and arrange and rearrange them on a sheet of white paper until an acceptable design is made, Fig. 42. Paste the pieces into place on the white paper. The design is now ready for cutting into waxed stencil board.

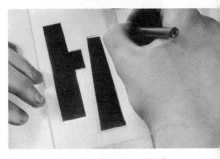

Fig. 43. Cut Slightly Beyond Square Corners

The Technique

1. Cut the stencil, making sure that keen, sharp cuts are made. Overlap the cuts lightly at the corners, Fig. 43.
2. Tack the cloth to a large board which has been covered with felt or several layers of muslin or news-

Fig. 44. Stretch Over Padded Board

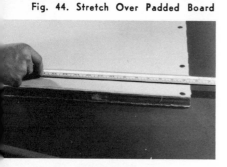

Fig. 45. Make Guide Line

paper. Be sure it is smooth and free of creases, Fig. 44.

3. Draw a line across the edge of the material (about two inches from the edge), using tailor's chalk and a yardstick, Fig. 45. It will be noted in the illustration that the edge of the material is unfinished. It is always better to finish the article after the decorating has been done, as would be the case if the material were purchased by the yard already decorated.

4. This line will serve as the guide line for the stencil as it is printed, Fig. 46.

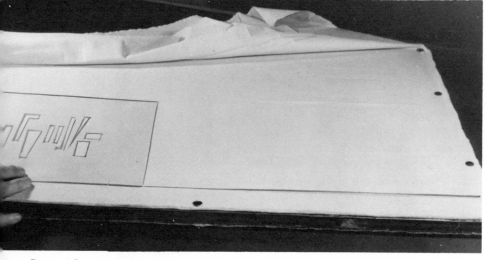

Fig. 46. Position Stencil on Line
Fig. 47. Mix Paint

5. Prepare the paint for stenciling. If one of the many excellent commercial varieties is used, it is important that the manufacturer's recommendations for mixing be followed. Many of them require the addition of the special mixers and extendors in varying proportions,

22

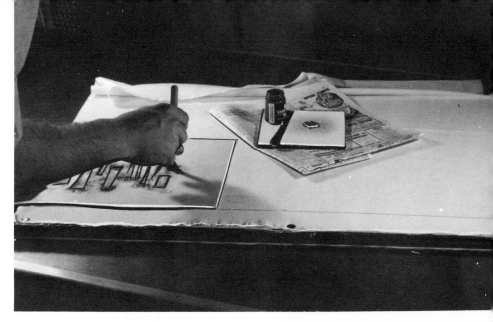

Fig. 48. Stencil First Print

depending upon the type of fabric, Fig. 47.

6. Place the stencil on the line and at the extreme left edge of the cloth. Apply the paint carefully with the stencil brush, Fig. 48.

7. Lift the stencil and place a sheet of plain white paper on top of the imprint precisely to the right-hand edge of the design, Fig. 49. This will prevent smudging the underside of the stencil when the next repeat is printed.

8. Place the stencil on the guide line again in the exact location to the right of the imprint just covered with paper, and stencil the second repeat, Fig. 50. Place a sheet of paper over this imprint, stencil the third imprint, and continue in this manner until the entire border has been printed.

9. Remove the cloth from the board, allow it to air dry for twenty-four

Fig. 49. Protect First Print With Paper

Fig. 50. Stencil Second Repeat

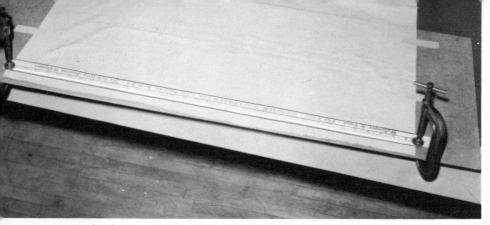

Fig. 51. Yardstick Forms Guide

hours, and then heat-set it for three minutes with a moderate iron. Hem the material and the curtains are complete as shown in Fig. 40.

Additional Hints

1. In the event the curtains have been purchased in finished condition and the border is to be placed close to the edge, a yard stick clamped down at both ends may be used as a "guide line" instead of the chalk line, Fig. 51.

2. It is extremely important that *new* fabric be washed completely free of starch and other "fillers" before being printed. After washing, the material must be ironed flat. Previously used materials which are to be printed should be thoroughly laundered first.

CHAPTER 5

Planning an Over-All Repeat

When decorating textiles, it is not long before it becomes necessary to plan a "repeat" pattern which will cover the entire area of the fabric, Fig. 52. Up until this point, the techniques have dealt with the spot design and the border repeat. Before attempting an over-all repeat, it is necessary to understand something of the *basic methods* used in developing such repeat patterns.

Fig. 52. Over-All Repeat Patterns

Fig. 53. Full Repeat Used in Apron
(Courtesy, Donna Gordon, New York)

Fig. 54. Planning Full Repeat

Fig. 55. Half-Drop Repeat

Types of Repeats

In general, there are three standard, evenly-spaced types of repeats. *Almost* every over-all repeat pattern which is seen will contain one or more of these three or *variations* of these three. The first is the *full repeat,* Fig. 53, in which the pattern *unit* is printed in even rows horizontally and vertically. As indicated in Fig. 54, in this type of repeat, the *unit* is constantly repeated without variation. The lines indicated in all of these drawings are considered *imaginary* but enable the artist to visualize the size and the amount of space available.

The second common type of repeat pattern is the *half-drop repeat,* Fig. 55. This is illustrated in the planning stage in the drawing depicted in Fig. 56. This particular pattern unit is about as simple as it is possible for the artist to create. It shows a geometric figure — in this case a circle. Each horizontal row of imprints is dropped one-half of an *imaginary box*. Note the spacing necessary between figures.

The third basic type of repeat is the *full drop repeat*. This is sometimes known as the diaper repeat, because of

Fig. 56. Planning Half-Drop Repeat

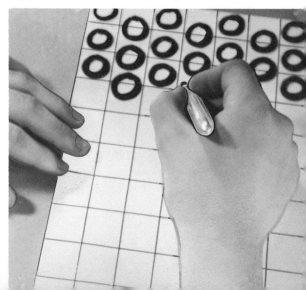

the *triangular* pattern which it creates to the eye as one views it, Fig. 57. In this variety, as depicted by the artist planning it in Fig. 58, the design *unit* is dropped a *full* imaginary box on alternate vertical rows. Many fabric designs indicate that the artist has utilized several of these basic techniques in one pattern or has used variations of some of them. Thus, there is the quarter-drop, three-quarter drop, etc. It is best for the beginner to be content with using the three *basic varieties*.

Fig. 57. Full-Drop Repeat

For Variety

Within any one of these repeat methods, additional variety may be created by *rotating, inverting,* or *reversing* the design unit. In *rotating*, the design is turned a quarter turn, either clockwise or counterclockwise, for each successive imprint so that it appears in the *original* imprint position each *fourth* imprint. This rotation may be developed either horizontally or vertically, Fig. 59.

Fig. 58. Planning Full-Drop Repeat

Fig. 59. Rotated Design

Fig. 60. Inverted Design

In the simple *inverting* method, the pattern unit is merely turned "upside down" for every alternate imprint, either vertically or horizontally, Fig. 60. A completely different perspective is frequently gained when the pattern unit is thus seen. In the *reversing* method, the design is turned *over* either to the left or to the right, so that it imprints in the position it would appear if viewed from behind the fabric, Fig. 61. This last method is not possible with all hand decorations on textiles, but with stenciling, the stencil is easily cleaned, turned over, and printed from the other side to obtain the effect desired.

Choosing Colors

The colors to be used for the decoration must also be chosen in advance and planned properly. (Reference is made to Chapter 19, "Colors and Color Mixing.") The individual artist or craftsman should choose the colors and color

28

combinations which are most satisfying. It is not the purpose of this section to lay down hard and fast rules governing color combinations. The following suggestions however, will prove helpful:

1. Consider the color of the material itself as *one* of the colors in the combination. Open areas in the design will admit this color "through."

2. Generally speaking, it is very difficult to apply *light* colors or white, *over* dark colors or black.

3. Consider the possibility of using *several shades or tints of one color* instead of always using two or more colors.

4. Very large, open designs frequently appear to *intensify the color* greatly. Therefore, it is usually advisable to use *shades or tints* of colors when decorating such areas.

5. Always consider the "white space" between design units as an integral part of the design itself. Great variety can be created by spacing the

Fig. 61. Reversed Design

units closer or farther apart regardless of the colors used. Notice the contrast in visual effect of the fabrics illustrated in Figs. 55 and 57. The circle has been used as the basic design. Different colors have been utilized, which is more apparent in the original than in the illustration. However, the *spacing* is what actually creates the dynamic element in the design. Where the design unit was printed closely together, one feels strength and solidity. Where the design unit was spaced with greater amounts of "white space" between each unit, a feeling of lightness and delicacy was created.

6. When applying colors to fabric, always work from "light to dark." Lighter colors are applied first; darker colors are applied after the lighter ones. *Darker colors* can be planned to "print over" certain areas of the lighter colors. The reverse of this is virtually impossible.

Planning the Repeat

A considerable amount of time should be given to planning the layout for an

Fig. 62. Rule Boxes

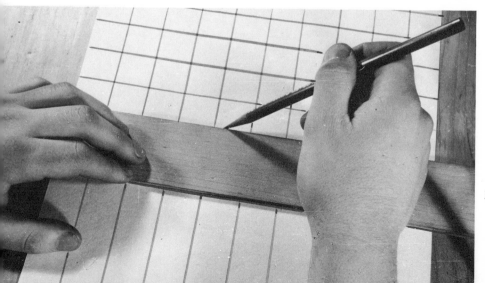

over-all repeat design, and this planning *must be done on paper*. The beginner, especially, is cautioned against developing a design and hastily applying it to the finished product. All too often the colors are not especially pleasant and the repeat motif is awkward and poorly spaced. *Neither* of these shortcomings can be corrected after the imprints have been made on the fabric.

The following simple steps, all carried out with pencil, paper, and scissors, will save countless hours of disappointment:

1. Develop the design unit, using any of the methods discussed in this text (cut paper, "scribbling," abstracting, etc.).
2. Cut, from stencil board, a temporary stencil of the design unit.
3. Rule off boxes on a *small* sheet of drawing paper. These will represent the *imaginary* areas in which the design unit will be printed, Fig. 62. These boxes are reduced in size for workability, but actually are used by the artist in planning the full size of the area and the design unit on the finished material.

Fig. 63. Plan Repeat

Fig. 64. Full-Size Layout Sheet

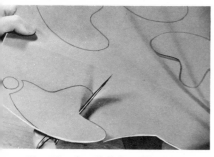

Fig. 65. Cut Full-Size Elements

Fig. 66. Paste Cut Outs in Place

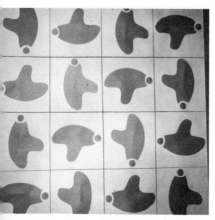

Fig. 67. Paper Replica

4. Using small discs of cardboard, arrange several rows in the *full* repeat, the *half-drop*, and the *full-drop* repeats, Fig. 63.

5. When the method of repeat has been determined, the artist is ready to lay out the design in the full, finished size. Take a large sheet of construction paper the approximate color of the color to be printed, and lay out (with very faint lines) the imaginary boxes. These should be the *full* size which they will be on the finished material, Fig. 64.

6. Using the temporary stencil (prepared in step two above), trace approximately a dozen outlines on construction paper of approximately the same color as the paint which will be used in the printing. Cut these out carefully with scissors, Fig. 65.

7. Arrange these cut outs in the boxes according to the repeat method decided upon, Fig. 66. Experiment with *rotating, inverting,* and *reversing* the unit. When the *precise arrangement* has been decided upon, paste the cut outs into place. The artist now has a paper replica of the finished material, Fig. 67. Except for slight variations in color shades or tints, it is an accurate presentation. Spacing, location of imprints, and other measurements can be taken from this paper plan.

CHAPTER 6

Over-All Repeat Patterns Stenciled in Two Colors

When planning an over-all stenciled repeat pattern, primary consideration must be given to the colors in which the stencils will be printed. For this particular project the over-all repeat pattern (used for draperies, slip covers, etc.) will be stenciled in *two* colors. Therefore it is necessary to cut *two* separate stencils. The design unit is developed by using the *geometric figure*

Fig. 68. Sketch Geometric Forms

Fig. 69. Cut Finished Forms

Fig. 70. Arrange Geometric Forms

Fig. 71. Assemble Arrangement

Fig. 72. Paste Shapes in Place

technique. Sketch four or five of the most common geometric forms on a sheet of paper, Fig. 68. Develop the forms into neat, finished shape, and cut them out of construction paper, Fig. 69.

The five geometric forms, Fig. 70, are then arranged one against the other until an acceptable combination is achieved, Fig. 71. Choose the colors for the different parts of the unit, as well as the color of the material on which the stenciling will take place. Cut each part of the design unit out of appropriately colored paper, assemble the complete unit, and paste it down on the proper colored paper, Fig. 72. The pattern unit is now ready for cutting into the stencil board.

Cutting the Stencils in Register

Take two sheets of stencil board (translucent variety), one for each color in the stencil, and place the pattern design on top of these, Fig. 73. Using a hand paper-punch, make three holes along the margin through *both* sheets

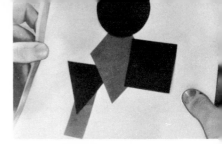

of stencil board *and* through the pattern sheet, simultaneously, Fig. 74. These holes will serve as "register" guides.

Fasten the pattern sheet down to the drawing board and fasten one sheet of the stencil board over it so that the three punched holes perfectly coincide or "register." Cut the stencil (as explained in Chapter 2) for the first, or lighter of the two colors, Fig. 75.

When completely cut, remove the stencil, but do *not* remove the pattern sheet. Fasten the second sheet of stencil board over the design so that the three register holes coincide with the three holes in the pattern sheet as before. Cut the second stencil for the darker of the two colors, Fig. 76. The two stencils are now cut in perfect register with the original design. In order to assure that a perfect imprint will be made and that a thin line of *unprinted area will not appear* between the colors, it is advisable that the stencil which will print the *darker color* be cut so that a thin portion of it overlaps the *lighter color* wherever the two colors meet.

Fig. 73. Assemble Stencils and Design

Fig. 74. Punch Register Holes

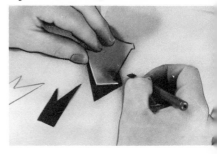

Fig. 75. Cut First Stencil

Fig. 76. Cut Second Stencil

Fig. 77. Arrange Final Layout

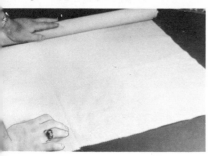

Fig. 78. Roll Cloth Around Tube

Using these two stencils, print a series of sample units with colored crayon or colored chalk as explained in Chapter 5. The colors should be the actual colors which will be used for the final printing. These paper imprints will be helpful in determining the *repeat sequence* and the final *layout* on a sheet of paper ruled off in large boxes, Fig. 77. This is explained fully in Chapter 5.

Preparing the Cloth

The length of cloth to be printed must be thoroughly laundered to remove all sizing or filler from the cloth. In the case of large pieces, this may be done in a washing machine. When ironing or pressing the cloth to remove the wrinkles, do not fold it when finished, but *roll* it around a tube made of newspaper. This will prevent creases from forming, Fig. 78.

When a long table is not available on which the length of fabric can be fastened for printing (in the manner in which it is printed professionally), the printing board, padded with felt or layers of newspaper as described in Chapter 4, may be used. This is not a disadvantage, except that the total area of cloth which can be printed at *one* "fastening-down" is limited by the size of the board used.

Fasten one end of the cloth to the board with tacks so that the *left* edge of the cloth is perfectly aligned with the *left* edge of the board, Fig. 79.

Laying Out on the Cloth

The distance between the *horizontal* rows is determined, Fig. 80, by placing the stencils over the paper layout. This measurement is marked off on both the *left and right edges* of the cloth with tailor's chalk, Fig. 81.

The actual distance between unit imprints, from left to right across the cloth, is measured with a ruler. A notation is made of this directly on the stencil board, Fig. 81. The artist will readily see the importance of the paper layout, since *all planning is done on it* and the measurements transferred to the actual printing surface.

Fig. 79. Stretch and Fasten Cloth

Fig. 80. Measure Horizontal Spacing

Fig. 81. Mark Horizontal Measure

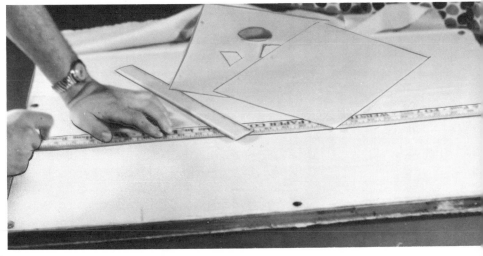

Fig. 82. Position Stencil

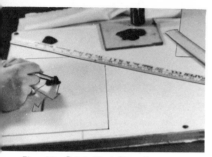

Fig. 83. Print First Stencil

Stenciling the First Color

To begin stenciling move the slab containing the paint (which has been properly prepared in advance) close to hand. Place the yardstick across the first set of marks on the two edges. Keep the left end of the yardstick in line with the left edge of the cloth and measure *toward the right* the proper distance at which to place the stencil for the *first color imprint*. This measurement is also taken from the paper layout, Fig. 82. Print the stencil, Fig. 83. It should be remembered that the lighter of the two colors is printed first. Continue in this fashion until all of the cloth which is stretched and fastened has been stenciled. Remove the printed section of cloth from the board, move the next section in place, fasten it to the board, and stencil it in the same manner. Continue this process until the entire length has been stenciled in the first color. After air-drying the cloth for several hours, the same process is repeated to stencil the *second* color. Fig. 84 shows the completed print.

There is always a question in the mind of the author at this stage in printing: is it more convenient to use the above process or is it better to allow the section of cloth which has been printed in the first color to air dry, and apply the second color printing to this area *before* changing the position of the cloth? This latter technique involves having several sets of colors prepared, cleaning stencils and brushes between colors, and waiting for each to dry to the touch before applying the next color. However, the cloth does not have to be fastened down

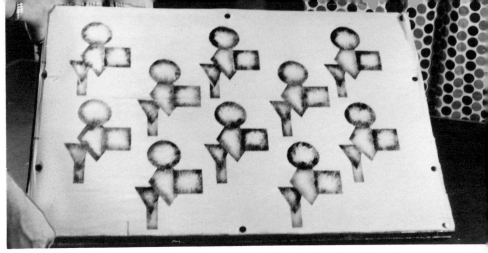

Fig. 84. Completed Print

more than once. The decision as to the technique used should depend upon the area of cloth which can be decorated at one time, and the drying speed of the paint.

Heat-Setting

When the stenciling is completed, the cloth is air-dried for twenty-four hours and then heat set. Since a large run of cloth which has been handled a great deal and marked with tailor's chalk will undoubtedly require an additional laundering before use, the following method of heat-setting (which does *not* simultaneously press the cloth) is more practical than using an electric iron:

1. Heat a *controllable* kitchen oven to 300 degrees Fahrenheit.
2. Gather the air dried cloth into a loose bunch. Do *not* fold it. Place the gathered cloth in a protective "basket" made of aluminum foil, Fig. 85.
3. Place it into the completely preheated oven, close the oven door, and allow it to remain for four or five minutes, Fig. 86. It is very important (especially when working with cotton and certain of the

Fig. 85. Prepare Foil Basket

Fig. 86. Heat-Set in Oven

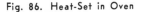

synthetic fabrics) that the oven temperature does not exceed 300 degrees Fahrenheit.

4. Launder the cloth (wash and press) in the usual manner.

Additional Hints

1. When more than a two-color stencil is required, the same procedure is used except that a stencil is cut for each color, resulting in as many stencils as there are colors.

2. Occasionally the advanced artist can accomplish stenciling in more than one color by using just *one* stencil. Usually in this case the color areas are widely enough separated in the design unit to enable brushing the paint only into those areas where it is desired. In other instances, *part* of the open area in the stencil is temporarily covered with a piece of blank stencil board while *one* color is being stenciled. It is advisable, especially for the beginner, to use a separate stencil for each color.

Additional References

Flam, David, *1001 Designs For Hand Decorating*. New York: Homecrafts, 1950.

Hallen, Julienne, *300 Projects For Hand Decorating*. New York: Homecrafts, 1950.

Moore, Edwena B., *Textile Painting*. San Diego: The Adept Litho Arts, 1949.

Now You Can Do It Yourself. Sandusky, Ohio: The American Crayon Co., n/d.

Stephenson, Jessie Bane, *From Old Stencils To Silk Screening*. New York: Charles Scribner's Sons, 1953.

Yates, Raymond F., *The Hobby Book of Stenciling and Brush-Stroke Painting*. New York: McGraw-Hill Book Co., 1951.

Zweybruck, Emmy, *The Second Stencil Book*. Sandusky, Ohio: The American Crayon Co., 1944.

CHAPTER 7

The Art of Batik

Batik is a resist-dye process, which is to say that it is one of the decorative techniques in which certain design areas are covered with a substance which will *resist* dyeing. After the fabric has been dyed, the resist substance is removed, leaving the color of the fabric showing through. The art was developed in the Orient, apparently in China or India, although the historic source is not known. It was developed to a high degree and is still practiced by the natives of Java. Fig. 87 illustrates an early 19th

Fig. 87. Batik - Early 19th Century (Courtesy, Metropolitan Museum of Art)

41

Fig. 88. Necktie Design Influenced by Batik

century Javanese Batik. Figs. 87a and 87b show native Indonesian women doing batik.

Design for Batik

The resist substance used in batik is a mixture of beeswax and paraffin. This is applied to the design areas. The material is dyed with a cold or warm, but not hot, dye so not to melt the wax resist. After the dye has dried, the wax is removed. Because molten wax is used to create the design areas, the individual artist has always been limited to a certain degree in the formation of the patterns. Molten wax, liquid in nature, imparts a liquid or "fluid" quality to the design.

Batik found its way into Europe when trade with the East was established, and it has had a strong influence on textile design ever since. Because of the fluid, freehand nature of the design, it enables the creative artist, as well as the ordinary craftsman, to apply his skill. In its original form, the batik was designed and executed directly on the cloth. In its relationship to other methods of textile decoration, batik has had a strong influence on the "tusche-glue" method of silk screen printing (described in a later chapter of this book). Many present-day fabric designs reflect this strong influence; for example, note the necktie pattern in Fig. 88.

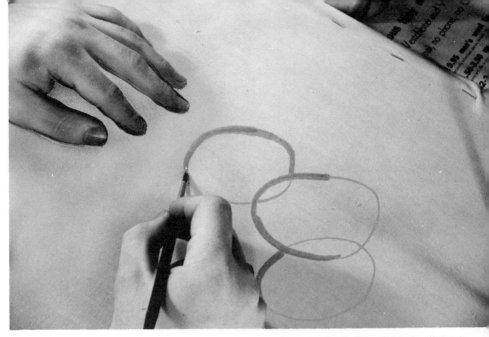

Fig. 89. Apply Wax With Small Brush

Tools and Equipment

Very few special tools or pieces of equipment are required for the practice of this art. In its simplest form, the artist merely applies molten wax to a stretched piece of fabric with a small brush, Fig. 89. When the wax has hardened, the piece of fabric is dyed in cold or lukewarm dye until the proper shade is desired, Fig. 90. Note that rubber gloves are worn to protect the hands against staining. After the dyed cloth is dried, it is placed between several sheets of heavy wrapping paper and pressed with a hot iron to remove the wax, Fig. 91. The design is now apparent in the area which was waxed and which resisted the dye action, Fig. 92.

Fig. 90. Dye Fabric

Fig. 92. Dyed Cloth

Fig. 91. Remove Wax

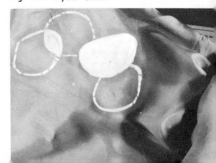

Fig. 93. Melt Beeswax and Paraffin

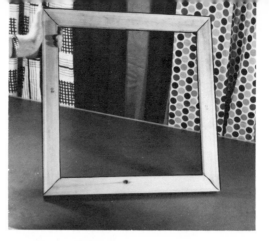

Fig. 94. Picture Frame Can Be Used

The wax resist is prepared by mixing equal parts (by weight) of household paraffin and beeswax (usually available under the name of dressmaker's beeswax). Place the paraffin and beeswax in a small double-boiler and heat until melted and blended, Fig. 93. This may then be cooled, broken into pieces, and remelted in the quantity desired as needed.

The frame used for stretching the fabric while applying the wax can be made from an ordinary picture frame or oil painting canvas frame, Fig. 94. Canvas or burlap aprons are tacked on the four sides of the frame, Fig. 95. The stretched cloth is attached to these aprons, thus giving the frame flexibility in adjusting to any piece of cloth *up to* the dimensions of the frame itself, Fig. 96.

Fig. 95. Tack Canvas Apron to Frame

Fig. 96. Aprons Give Flexible Size

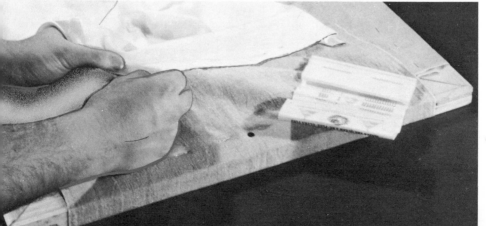

Fig. 97. Tjanting Tool

A professional *tjanting tool* may be purchased from an art supply firm, Fig. 97. This is an adaptation of the original Javanese tool used for applying the molten wax. It consists of a metal cup attached to a wooden handle. The cup has a thin spout leading from its base, through which the wax flows while being applied. Fig. 98 shows the method of holding the tjanting while applying the wax. An interesting substitute for this tool is found in an ordinary oil can, Fig. 99.

The dyes may be purchased commercially in powdered form, Fig. 100a, or in liquid form. Equally as good a substance to use is *waterproof* drawing ink. This is available in a wide variety of colors and is washproof after it has dried, Fig. 100b.

Fig. 98. Manner of Holding Tool

Fig. 99. Using Oil Can Substitute

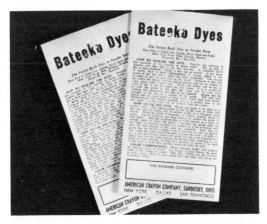

Fig. 100a. Powdered Batik Dyes (Courtesy, American Crayon Company)

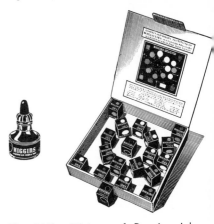

Fig. 100b. Waterproof Drawing Ink (Courtesy, Higgins Ink Co., Inc.)

Fig. 101. Lay Out Design on Paper

Fig. 102. Color Areas With Chalk

The Technique

1. Choose a design or develop one which gives a fluid, freehand appearance. The *scribbling method*, discussed in Chapter 3, is an ideal method to use in developing a batik design.

2. Lay out the design on a sheet of drawing paper, Fig. 101, and fill in the areas with soft, colored chalk, Fig. 102. In any usual dyeing process, of which batik is one, the colors are transparent. This means that one color dyed over another will produce a *third* color. This characteristic of "over-dyeing" is used to advantage in the batik process because just *two* successive dyeings will produce *three* colors on the final product. When using soft chalk for the planning stage, the colors may be blended with the fingertip, Fig. 103, to produce the secondary color. (Refer to Chapter 19, "Colors and Color Mixing.")

46

3. The artist must remember to work from light colors to dark colors, and in the batik process, from the primary colors (red, yellow, and blue) to the secondary colors (orange, green, and violet). Thus, a piece of *white* cloth can be decorated in as many as *eight* colors (including the basic white) by dyeing in just *three* dye baths. Blue dyed over yellow will produce green, and blue dyed over red will produce violet. Red dyed over yellow will produce orange. The combination of all three primary colors will produce brown, while those areas resisted with wax throughout *all* of the dyeing process will remain white. An understanding of this relationship of colors is probably the most difficult part of the batik process, but is also *that* part of the process which gives the artist the greatest variety in applying his skill.

Fig. 103. Blend Colors With Fingertip

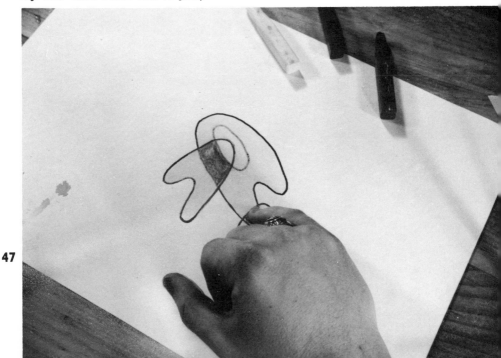

4. Prepare the fabric by washing it thoroughly and ironing it free of all creases. Silk and sheer cottons are most adaptable to this process because they are thin and permit the wax to permeate completely.

5. Stretch the fabric on the frame as previously explained.

6. Transfer the design to the fabric. The use of ordinary pencil or tailor's chalk is *not recommended* for this process because these materials are sometimes difficult to remove from the fibers of the cloth. In the batik process, where most areas are successively covered with wax and dyes, the problem of removing unwanted lines becomes a serious problem. Two methods of transferring the design are suggested:

   a. Cut the design outline from heavy paper. Using this as a pattern, trace around it with a stick of ordinary blackboard chalk which has been pointed with sandpaper, Fig. 104. The chalk powder thus deposited will be readily washed out in the dye bath.

Fig. 104. Outline Design

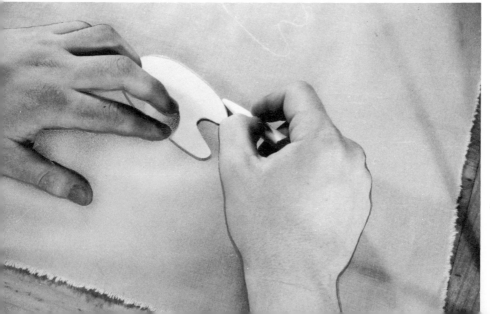

b. Trace the design onto thin tracing paper and then punch small holes along the lines of the design with either a large darning needle, Fig. 105, or a "pouncing wheel," Fig. 106. Place the pattern over the fabric and using a small wad of absorbent cotton, rub draftsman's *pouncing powder* or talcum powder through the holes, Fig. 107. This will produce a tracing of the pattern in a dotted line which is easily followed when applying the wax. When working on a pure white cloth, the pouncing powder or talcum may be mixed into a paste with a few drops of vegetable food coloring. Do this several hours before using, then when the paste is dry, mash it into a powder again. Color the powder sufficiently to produce enough contrast to the white cloth.

7. Apply the wax, using the tjanting tool (which is most applicable to fine line work) or the oilcan, or the brush (for heavy, fill-in work.)

Fig. 105. Punch Holes With Needle

Fig. 106. Use Pouncing Wheel

Fig. 107. Rub Powder Through Holes

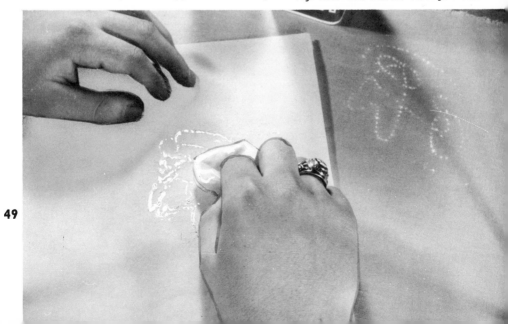

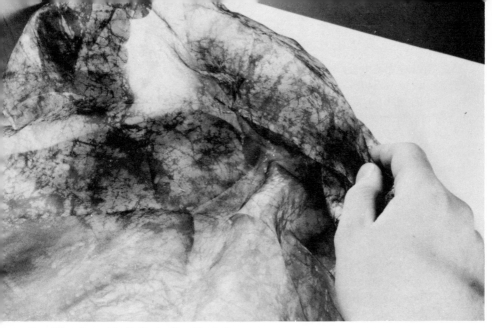

Fig. 108. Over-All, Delicate Crackle Pattern

Fig. 109. Wax Entire Cloth

8. Allow the wax to dry thoroughly. This may be hastened by holding the fabric under cold water. Care must be taken at this stage that the *wax is not cracked.* Such cracks will admit dye through to the cloth and result in a "crackle" following the line of the crack in the wax. The higher the percentage of paraffin in the beeswax-paraffin mixture, the greater the tendency there will be for the wax to crack. Temperature also will govern the results. If the workroom is cold, or if the work is plunged into cold water, there will be more likelihood of the wax cracking.

Some artists, however, deliberately produce a *crackle* to their batik. Fig. 108 illustrates an over-all, delicate crackle pattern. This is produced by waxing the entire piece of cloth, Fig. 109. When the wax has dried, the cloth is crumpled into a ball between the hands, Fig. 110. It is then immersed in the dye bath. When the wax is removed, the fine veining of color is apparent wherever there were cracks in the wax.

9. Special batik dyes or waterproof drawing inks are used for dyeing the waxed cloth, because heat cannot be used in the dye bath lest the wax melt, ruining the pattern. In most cold water dye baths, the intensity of the color is increased as the cloth is allowed to remain in the bath for a longer time. In this manner, a wide variety of tints can be produced.

10. When the dyeing is completed, the work is removed and dried.

11. After drying, the wax is removed by pressing the cloth between sheets of brown wrapping paper. Use a hot iron as previously described. If the artist has a well-ventilated area in which to work, the wax may be removed by washing the cloth in gasoline or naphtha benzine until the wax is completely dissolved. These solvents do not affect the coloration of the dye.

Fig. 110. Crumple Waxed Cloth

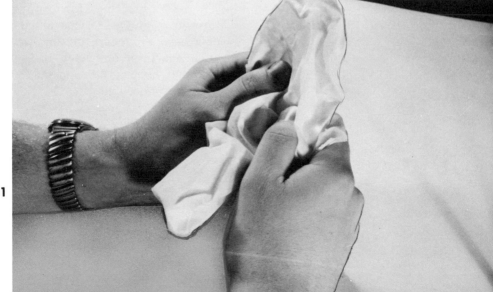

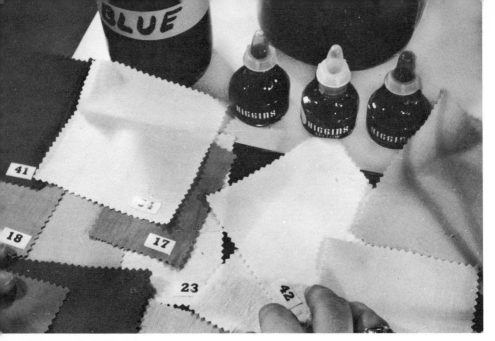

Fig. 111. Code Dyed Swatches for Reference

Additional Hints

1. Always be sure when planning designs for batik, that fluid, soft-flowing patterns are chosen. There is no point, artistically, in creating a batik which can just as readily be accomplished in stencil or block print.

2. It is advisable to dye sample swatches of material in the various dye baths which will be used and to label these swatches for future reference, Fig. 111. Some artists even record the length of time the swatch has been immersed in the dye so that various tints and shades can be reproduced at will.

CHAPTER 8

A Batik Handkerchief

A few words of repetition may be worthwhile at this point. Always keep in mind the successive color applications when planning and designing a multi-color batik. If the fabric is white at the beginning, then all areas which are waxed and dyed in the first dye bath will be white when the wax has been removed. If yellow is the first dye bath, as it most usually is, then the entire cloth will be dyed yellow except for those areas resisted with the wax.

The artist must keep four colors in mind as he applies wax before dyeing the second color. For example, if red is the second color to be applied, it will convert white to red and yellow to orange. Upon removal of this second application of wax then, there will be areas of white, yellow, orange and red if the wax is applied to take advantage of all possibilities.

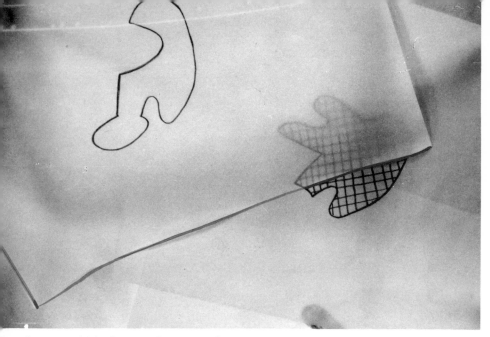

Fig. 112a. Make Separate Tracings on Tissue

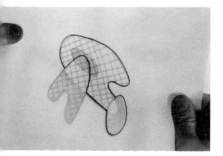

Fig. 112b. Check Register of Tracings

Procedure

1. Develop the design and plan the colors on paper, using colored chalk as described in the preceding chapter. For further accuracy in determining the color areas, *three* tracings of the pattern may be drawn on thin tracing paper, one for the yellow areas, one for the red areas, and one for the blue areas. When these are held together with light shining through them, the artist can actually see each color area, including those to be produced by second and third successive dyeings, Figs. 112a, 112b.

2. Prepare the fabric by thorough laundering. Use white cloth with unfinished edges. These are finished after all dyeing is complete. Stretch the cloth to the frame.

3. Transfer the design to the cloth. Wax in all areas which are *not* to

be dyed in the first color, Fig. 113. Remembering that dyeing is always accomplished from the lighter to the darker colors, it is recommended that the sequence of dyeing be yellow, then red, then blue. Therefore, in this first waxing, all areas which have *not* been covered with wax will be dyed yellow.

4. Dye the cloth to the proper intensity. Allow it to dry and remove the wax. The areas previously waxed will now appear as white, Fig. 114.

5. Stretch the cloth again and wax in those areas which are to resist the second color (red), Fig. 115. It must be remembered now that those white areas which are covered with wax will remain white throughout this red dyeing, and those yellow areas which are covered with wax will remain yellow. The white areas which are *not wax resisted* will become red, and the yellow areas which are *not waxed* will become orange.

6. After dyeing in red and drying, the wax is removed, disclosing *three* colors (in addition to white) after just *two* dye baths, Fig. 116.

Fig. 113. Apply Wax for First Dye

Fig. 114. Waxed Areas Remain White

Fig. 115. Wax for Second Dye

Fig. 116. Three Colors; Two Dyeings

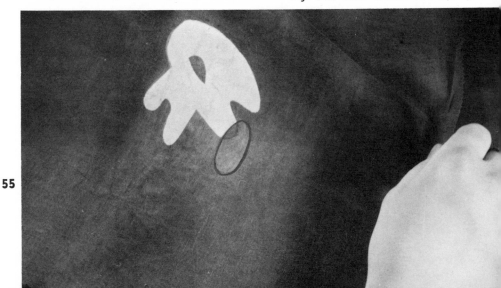

7. Once again the cloth is stretched on the frame and those areas which are to *resist* the third color bath (blue) are waxed in.

8. After dyeing in blue and thoroughly drying, it will be noted that a new series of colors has appeared, Fig. 117. Where the blue dyed over white, the cloth has become blue, where it has dyed over red it has become violet, where it has dyed over yellow it has become green, and where it has dyed over orange it has become brown.

9. Remove the wax thoroughly and the final design is revealed, showing a total of seven colors in addition to white, Fig. 118. In the case of this handkerchief, only the background was permitted to become colored in brown.

10. Launder the cloth in lukewarm water and mild soap, press, hem the edges, and the batik project is complete.

Fig. 119 illustrates a few typical batik designs, mostly of a traditional nature.

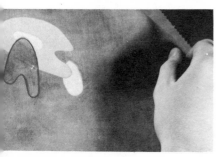

Fig. 117. Cloth After Blue Dyeing

Fig. 118. Finished Design

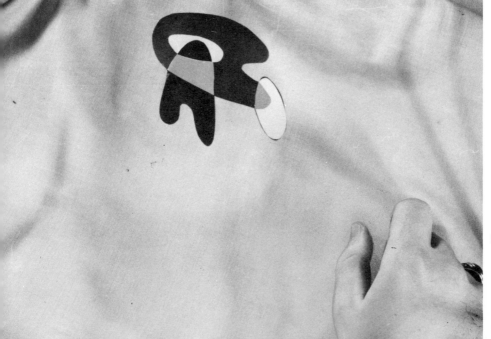

Additional References

Mijer, Peter, *Batiks and How To Make Them.*
New York: Dodd Mead & Co., 1919.

Parisi, Tony, *Craftsmen's Instruction Handbook.* New York: Educational Materials,
Inc., 1945.

Fig. 119. Typical Batik Designs (Courtesy, **Textile Decorating,** by Pedro deLemos)

CHAPTER 9

Tie Dyeing

Fig. 120. Tie and Dye with Embroidery on Damask (Courtesy, Metropolitan Museum of Art)

Tie dyeing is another of the unusual and specialized techniques developed by man for the decoration of fabric. It was undoubtedly conceived in Central India or on the island of Bali (where it is still practiced) and subsequently introduced into the Orient. Fig. 120 illustrates a classic example of this fine art from Japan (18th century).

Design for Tie Dyeing

In essence, tie dyeing is the process of tying certain portions of fabric with thread or string prior to dyeing it. After dyeing, the ties are removed, disclosing un-dyed areas in the form of patterns resulting from the ties. Fig. 121 indicates the variety of *simple* designs which can be created by varying the method of tying. These will be explained later in the chapter. In the upper left-hand corner of this piece of silk are several small circular designs, with larger ones directly below. To the right of these is a semi-rectangular design made up of concentric figures, while the upper and lower right-hand corners depict typical corner devices.

The technique of tie dye has had its influence in textile design throughout the ages and is felt in many bold contemporary designs. The silk scarf held by the artist in Fig. 122 and shown in use in Fig. 123 is an example of a simple, basic treatment with the tie dye technique. The place mat in Fig. 124 shows another application of this primitive method of dyeing.

Fig. 124. Tie Dyed Place Mat

Fig. 121. Simple Designs for Tie Dyeing

Fig. 122. Tie Dyed Scarf

Fig. 123. Simple Motif Is Effective

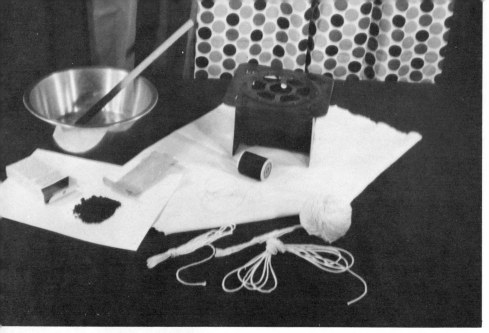

Fig. 125. Materials and Equipment

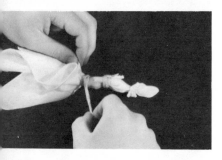

Fig. 126. Tying Rosette Pattern

Fig. 127. Dyed Rosette

Basic Techniques

The actual technique of tie dyeing is simple and flexible. Basically, this chapter will deal with just three broad varieties of tie dye patterns. These are the *rosette*, the *broad stripe*, and the *fine repeat*. The materials and equipment necessary for the application of the art are simple (Fig. 125). These consist of several weights of thread, twine, and cord (including plumber's cord or lampwick, which is a soft, stranded cord used for covering wide areas); a stainless steel, agate, or glass vessel for dyeing, with a wood stirring stick; commercially prepared, boilable dye; a source of heat; the fabric to be dyed.

The *rosette* pattern is created by tying two or more bands around a circularly gathered portion of cloth as shown on the handkerchief in Fig. 126. The resulting pattern after dyeing and removal of the ties is illustrated in Fig. 127. The *broad stripe* (shown in applied use in Fig. 123) is created by rolling the fabric and tying bands tightly in those areas which are to resist the dye, Fig. 128. The pattern is disclosed after dyeing and removal of the ties, Fig. 129. This application can be applied to an entire length of fabric, as later explained. The *fine repeat* is developed by tying small, pointed bunches of the fabric wherever the repeat pattern is desired, Fig. 130. After dyeing and removal of the ties, the pleasantly repeated pattern is disclosed, Fig. 131. It should be remembered that the finer the thread or twine used, the more delicate the resulting pattern. Bold patterns are created by using heavy twine or cord and tying up larger areas.

Fig. 128. Tying for Broad Stripe

Fig. 129. Dyed Broad Stripe

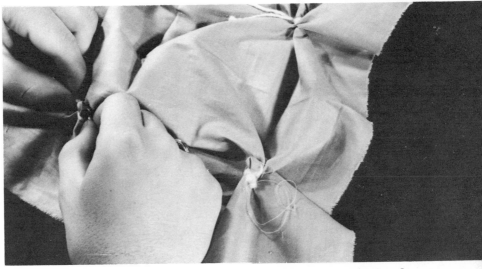

Fig. 130. Tying for Fine Repeat

Fig. 131. Dyed Repeat

61

Fig. 132. Heating With Alcohol Stove

Fig. 133. Heating With Bunsen Burner

Fig. 134. Rinse Until Water Is Clear

Dyeing

The dye bath should be prepared according to the manufacturer's directions. Most present-day commercial (home type) dyes do not require the use of a mordant (a chemical substance which when combined with a dyestuff produces a fixed color). When mordants *are called for* in the directions, they usually consist of common table salt or vinegar. The dye should be mixed in a non-corrosive vessel such as glass, stainless steel, or agate. The dye bath may be heated over a simple, solidified alcohol type of stove, Fig. 132, or it may be heated over a bunsen burner, Fig. 133. It most certainly may be heated over a common kitchen range.

After the fabric has been properly tied, it is thoroughly moistened, immersed in the dye bath, and dyed according to manufacturer's recommendations. Most dyes are flexible to the extent that a shorter dyeing time will result in tints but some dyes will be colorfast only when dyed to full intensity.

After the dyeing is completed, the fabric should be rinsed in cold, running water until no dye bleeds from the material, Fig. 134. (Note that the artist is wearing rubber gloves for protection against skin stains and possible allergic reactions.) The ties are then removed, and the fabric is dried. It should then be washed in warm water with a mild soap and pressed while damp.

In planning for single color and multi-color dying, as with batik, (Chapters 7 and 8) it must be remembered that the dyes are transparent. For working pur-

62

poses, this means that one color dyed over another will result in a third color. Since tie dye is an *extremely free technique,* the pattern layouts cannot be planned too precisely. However, some planning must be accomplished by the artist so that patterns fall within certain areas and the colors create the harmony desired.

Dyeing Yard Goods

An interesting application of the tie dye technique is in dyeing large runs of material which can be converted into drapes, slip covers, and even dresses. In planning such a project, the artist draws the rough sketch on a sheet of paper with soft colored chalk, blocking in the desired colors and patterns, Fig. 135. The only modification in the actual process is that more time will be required for the tying, more string or cord and more dye will be used, and a larger dyeing vessel will be necessary.

Fig. 135. Plan With Colored Chalk

63

Fig. 136. Cross-Tied Dyeing Gives
Seven Colors With Three Dyeings

Fig. 136 shows a length of material dyed in the three primary colors, resulting in seven separate colors plus white. (See Chapter 7 for a complete explanation of the results of over-dyeing, and Chapter 19, "Colors and Color Mixing.") The material shown in the illustration was originally white. It was tied horizontally, using the *broad stripe* technique. It was then dyed yellow. When the ties were removed, the areas which resisted the dye remained white while the remainder of the cloth was yellow. It was then tied up again, horizontally, so that the ties covered some white *and* yellow areas. It was dyed in a blue dye bath. After untying, the fabric contained blue and green areas as well as white and yellow. It was blue where the blue dye struck the white cloth and green where the blue dye struck the yellow cloth.

It was then tied a *third* time. For this third tie up, the ties were made *across* the material, vertically, using the same *broad stripe* technique. It was then dyed in a red dye bath. Red dyed over the white areas produced red; over the blue areas, violet; over the yellow areas, orange. Where all three basic dye baths covered the same area, a rich brown resulted. In this manner a soft, fluid, subtle over-all pattern was produced in seven colors *and* white by dyeing the cloth just three times. Between each tying and dyeing, the cloth was rinsed, untied, and dried as previously explained.

Fig. 137. Over-All Repeat Pattern

Additional Hints

1. An interesting variation in an over-all repeat pattern in tie dye can be obtained by using blocks of wood in addition to tying with cord, Fig. 137. The cloth is folded into even rectangles, first horizontally and then vertically, Fig. 138. A block of wood is placed on either side of this folded pile and the cord is tied around both the cloth and the blocks, Fig. 139.

Fig. 138. Fold Both Ways

2. Generally speaking, all ties are made rather tightly to insure that the dye does not "bleed" through the ties into the areas which are intended to resist dye. However, deliberately tying loosely frequently results in an unusual and unpredictable pattern.

3. Another interesting technique is the *variegated pattern*. The cloth to be dyed is gathered into a loose bunch. The cord or twine is

Fig. 139. Tie Blocks on Either Side

wrapped around haphazardly as a length of yarn is wound into a ball. The material is then dyed.

4. Since tie dye is a relatively loose, free, and unpredictable technique, as described herein, the artist would do well to maintain a sampler such as shown in Fig. 140, with accompanying notes so that patterns which *have* been developed can be repeated later on with a fair degree of accuracy.

Additional References

Charm of Color, The. Quincy, Illinois: Monroe Chemical Co., 1948.

Information File On Home Dyeing. New York: Tintex Home Economics Bureau, 1957.

Parisi, Tony, *Craftsman's Instruction Handbook.* New York: Educational Materials, Inc., 1945.

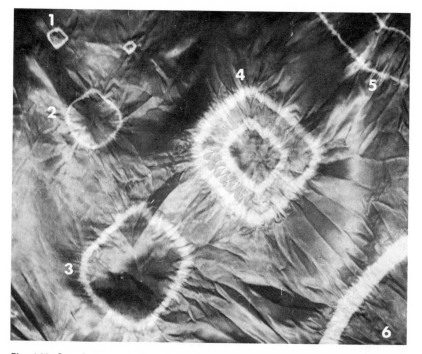

Fig. 140. Sampler
1. Fine Repeats, Tied with Thread. 2. Single Rosette, Thread Used. 3. Rosette, from Cord. 4. Rosette, Two Tyings. 5. Corner Tying, Fine Thread. 6. Corner Tying, Heavy Twine.

CHAPTER 10

Linoleum Block Printing

Block printing, unlike most other techniques for applying design, involves the use of a block or plate into which the design has been cut or carved. This carved block is covered with ink and the design is transferred to the printing surface by stamping.

In the application of the art a design is carefully cut into the surface of a thick piece of linoleum, Fig. 141. This is then mounted with glue and small

Fig. 141. Remove Non-Printing Areas

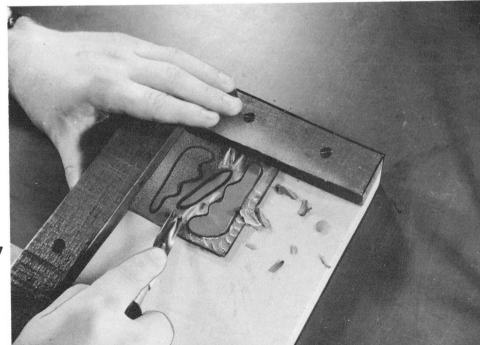

Fig. 142. Mount Linoleum

nails to a sturdy block of wood, Fig. 142. The surface is inked thoroughly by applying ink from a roller, Fig. 143. The inked surface is applied to the cloth and printed under pressure — in this case by striking the back with a mallet, Fig. 144. The design is thus transferred to the cloth, Fig. 145.

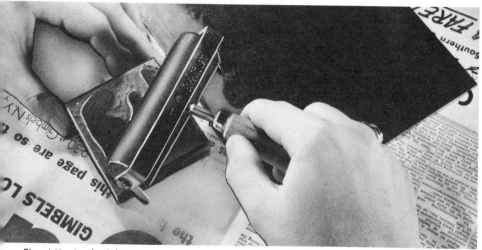

Fig. 143. Apply Ink

Fig. 144. Strike With Mallet

Fig. 145. Completed Print

Fig. 146. Block Prints — Germany, 12th Century (Courtesy, Metropolitan Museum of Art)

Figs. 147a and b. Contemporary Block Prints

Fig. 148. Rubber Stamp and Engraved Plate

Fig. 146 shows a variety of 12th century German block prints. The blocks used were painstakingly carved of hard wood. Figs. 147a and 147b illustrate several modern block-printed fabric samples in which linoleum blocks were utilized. Fig. 148 shows two modern applications of the ancient art of block printing. One is the common rubber stamp used so frequently; the other is an electroplate, or minutely engraved copper plate used for printing photographs on paper. Historically, the artist's block print was the forerunner of printing. Samples of block prints from as early as the 8th and 9th centuries have been found in China and Japan. It remained for other men, hundreds of years later, to discover that the letters of the alphabet could be carved into wood and imprinted on paper.

Tools and Equipment

The tools and materials needed are few and inexpensive. The linoleum used may be any heavy variety; a solid color is best. The grade known as "battleship" linoleum is most often used. White battleship linoleum in small squares and rectangles, unmounted or already mounted on wooden blocks, can be purchased in a variety of sizes in local art stores, Fig. 149.

Fig. 149. Linoleum

Fig. 150a. Simple Set of Cutters

There are many varieties of cutting tools — from the simple, inexpensive set shown in Fig. 150a to a very complete set of carving tools, Fig. 150b. Any set consisting of one handle with interchangeable blades is recommended for the beginner.

A wide assortment of oil-base, block-printing inks is available commercially, Fig. 151. For the artist who has already invested in tube oils, there are several excellent "mixing compounds" which, when added to the oil paint, create color-fast, washproof paint. *Mixo*, manufactured by the F. Weber Co., and *Textine*, manufactured by M. Grumbacher, Inc., are two of these materials. Printer's ink, mixed with the special acetic acid mordant explained in Chapter 2, may also be used. Any of these materials must be mixed to a heavier consistency when used for block printing than when used for various other types of application. *Prang Textile Paint,* manufactured by The American Crayon Co., is especially suited to all types of textile decoration. A special *block printing extendor* is available, which when correctly added to the basic paint, gives a block printing medium of perfect consistency and vis-

Fig. 150b. Carving Tools (Courtesy, M. Grumbacher, Inc.)

Fig. 151. Oil-Base, Block-Printing Inks

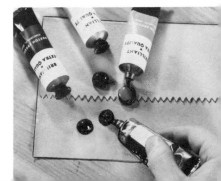

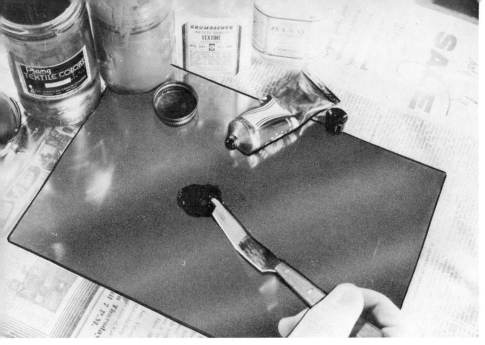

Fig. 152. Mix to Manufacturer's Directions

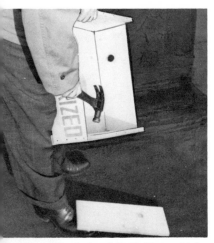

Fig. 153. Ends of Fruit Crates Make Satisfactory Blocks

Fig. 154. Improvised Cutting Tool

cosity. It is highly recommended that all of these materials be used according to the manufacturer's recommendations. Fig. 152.

The thick ends of discarded fruit and tomato crates make excellent blocks of wood for mounting the linoleum, Fig. 153. An improvised cutting tool can be made from a steel umbrella rib by cutting it off square, sharpening it to a bevel edge, and mounting it in a standard wood file handle, Fig. 154.

The mallet is the most practical of all tools for creating the pressure required to "print" the block impression. However, other devices may be used as well. When it is possible to hold the printing block in a "face up" position and place the fabric being printed *on top of* the printing block, a rolling pin may be used to give the pressure. It is merely rolled across the cloth, pressing it against the inked block, Fig. 155. An

72

Fig. 155. Rolling Pin

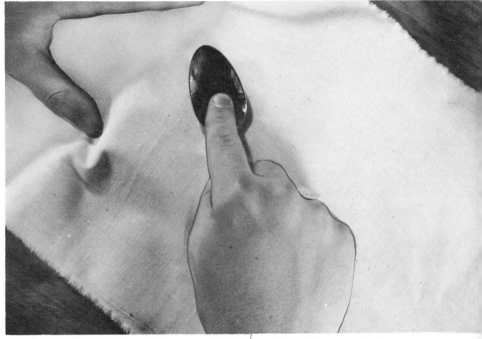

Fig. 156. Spoon Bowl

ordinary teaspoon can be used as well, when the block and cloth are in this same position. The spoon is rubbed vigorously across the cloth, Fig. 156, pressing it against the inked block. Foot pressure is used frequently in printing large pieces of cloth. The cloth is spread out on the floor; the inked block set in the proper place; and the artist steps on the block, using the weight of his body to create the pressure needed for printing. Fig. 157. The rubber roller (Fig. 168) is an important device, though the block *can* be inked with a brush.

Fig. 157. Foot Pressure

The Technique

1. Develop a design which will be applicable to the block printing method. Block prints should always have a massive, bulky appearance. Once again the craftsman is cautioned against executing a design with a technique *not compatible* with the characteristics of the design. The "scribbling" technique explained in Chapter 3, the "cut paper" technique explained in Chapter 4, or the "geometric" technique explained in Chapter 6, are all good methods to use in developing designs for block printing. The beginner should keep his design unit within approximately a four by six inch area. The design unit which has been decided upon should then be drawn to full scale and dimensions, Fig. 158.

2. In block printing it is customary to decide upon one of three basic design applications, *after* the design unit itself has been chosen.

Fig. 158. Draw to Full Scale

Fig. 159. Possible Applications

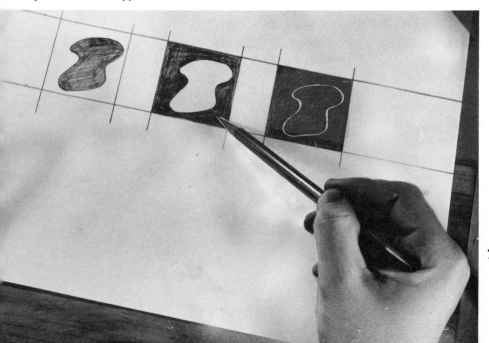

These three basic design applications are the *positive rendering* of the design, the *negative rendering*, and the *fine line*. It will be noted in Fig. 159 that a simple form has been rendered in these three applications by the artist. The first, from the left, illustrates the positive technique in which the design motif itself will be printed in color and all of the background will be *unprinted* — will remain the color of the cloth being printed. The second box on the drawing illustrates the negative, or opposite application. Here the *design motif will not be printed* and thus will appear in the color of the cloth, while the *entire background* will be printed. The third of the methods, the fine line, consists of *outlining* in a fine line *the entire dimension and shape* of the design motif. This outline will appear in the color of the cloth while the remaining area will be printed.

Fig. 160. Trace in Reverse

3. The decision has been made, for purposes of illustration, to render the design unit shown in Fig. 158 in the positive application for block printing. It is then traced in outline, *in reverse*, Fig. 160. This reversal operation is extremely important in all relief printing processes. If the artist begins work with a drawing of a profile which faces to the left, traces this onto a linoleum block and cuts it out, it will then print with the profile facing to the *right*. It will be recalled that rubber stamps and type

used for printing all appear in reverse. Therefore, if the printed design is to appear in the same position as the original drawing, the block *must* be cut in reverse. There are some designs in which this is not very important (geometric designs) but most freeform designs change in visual aspect when the directional dynamics are changed. Reversing a design is accomplished very simply by placing a sheet of carbon paper, *carbon side up,* under the design and drawing over the design with a hard pencil. The carbon will transfer the design onto the back of the drawing sheet in *reverse.*

4. Trace this outline onto a rectangle of linoleum slightly larger than the design, Fig. 161. Carbon paper may also be used for this tracing, or the back of the drawing may be covered with heavy pencil markings or chalk. When the design is being traced, the layer of pencil marking or chalk will act in the same manner as carbon paper and transfer the design to the linoleum.

5. Using drawing ink, fill in *all printing areas* of the design on the linoleum. These are the areas which will *not be cut out* of the linoleum, Fig. 162.

6. Cut away all areas on the linoleum which are *not inked in,* Fig. 163. It is best, when cutting, to first cut with a fine veining tool, an outline around the entire area to be cut away. Use a fine "V" shape gouge. Next, the larger "V" shape

Fig. 161. Trace Design onto Linoleum

Fig. 162. Fill In Printing Areas

76

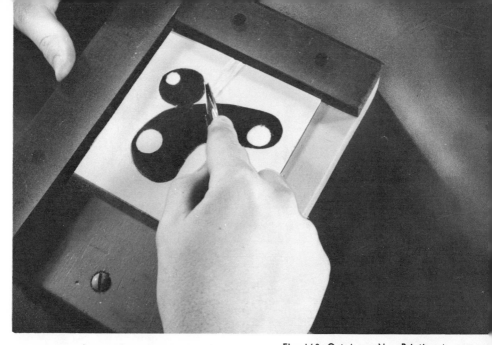

Fig. 163. Cut Away Non-Printing Areas

gouge is used, going over the same cuts, but cutting into the unwanted areas rather than into the design areas. Finally, a heavy gouge ("U" shape gouge) is used to cut out all unwanted areas of the linoleum. The cut should be about half the thickness of the linoleum, although cuts which extend clear through to the burlap backing are not uncommon in practice, providing they do not weaken or separate portions of the linoleum.

It will be noted in Fig. 163 that the artist is using a specially constructed "bench hook" for safety in cutting. This is a common bench hook used by carpenters, except that an additional strip of wood has been fastened along the left edge, Fig. 164. This, plus the backing strip, enables the artist to hold the linoleum block against the back edge or left-hand edge and to use the cutter in such a manner that

Fig. 164. Bench Hook

Fig. 165. Nail in Non-Printing Areas

the *non-cutting hand* will not have to be placed in front of the blade to hold the block. There is always some danger that the knife will slip while cutting. If the non-cutting hand is in front of the line of cut, injury may occur.

7. Mount the linoleum on a block of wood the same size as the piece of

Fig. 166. Mark Register Points on Cloth

linoleum. Animal glue may be used for attaching, or small nails (with heads) may be used. Drive the nails through areas of the linoleum which have been cut away for non-printing, Fig. 165.

8. Using the edges of the wooden block as a guide, place small strips of gummed tape on the cloth to be printed, properly located where the imprints are to be made, Fig. 166.

Fig. 167. Ink the Block

These strips of tape are called "register" marks.

9. Ink the block, Fig. 167. It is advisable to invest in an inexpensive rubber roller for this purpose, similar to the one shown in Fig. 168. However, the ink or paint can be dabbed onto the block with a small piece of cloth, Fig. 169, or evenly applied with a small, soft brush.

10. Using a small piece of clean cloth, wipe away any paint which may have been deposited on areas of the linoleum which are not intended to

Fig. 168. Rubber Roller or Brayer (Courtesy, M. Grumbacher, Inc.)

Fig. 169. Cloth May Be Used

Fig. 170. Position Block

print. Place the block in the printing position (linoleum surface down) on the cloth, against the register marks, Fig. 170, and print it, using a mallet. Do not slide the inked block across the cloth, but place it precisely where it is to print.

11. Remove the block, and the print is finished, Fig. 171.

12. After the prints have air dried, heat-set them as explained in Chapter 2.

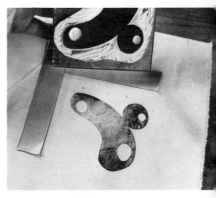

Fig. 171. Finished Print

Fig. 172. Launder Fabric After Heat-Setting (Courtesy, Westinghouse Electric Corp.)

Fig. 173. Rotated Border Repeat

Fig. 174. Over-All Repeat Pattern — Note Register Marks

13. Following the heat-setting, thoroughly launder the fabric. This is usual practice in all techniques involving the application of a paint or ink to the surface of the fabric to remove any excess bits of the paint which have not fused into the fibers. This laundering may be accomplished in a washing machine if the piece of fabric is too large to conveniently hand launder, Fig. 172.

14. When the printing is complete, clean the linoleum of paint with a cloth moistened in kerosene or benzine.

Repeat Printing

Border repeats and over-all repeats can be accomplished in block printing through the same planning process explained in Chapter 5. The reader is reminded, however, that reverse prints are *not possible* with block printing because there is but *one possible printing surface*. It is possible to rotate the block, either clockwise or counterclockwise, to add variety to the repeat pattern.

Imprints are made on paper, cut out, and assembled in the desired repeat motif as discussed in Chapter 5. The measurements are then transferred to the cloth using small strips of tape for register marks as in step 8, above. The printing is then made as described, but remember that the block has to be inked before each imprint is made. Remove all strips of tape before heat-setting or laundering. Fig. 173 shows a border repeat being made using a clockwise rotation of the pattern.

Over-all repeats are accomplished in the same manner. Remember to fasten the cloth to a printing board so that register marks are accurately made, Fig. 174.

Additional Hints

1. All fabric used for decorating, regardless of the technique, should be clean, thoroughly free from sizing, and pressed flat.

2. Single imprints or spot design technique, using the linoleum block method, can usually be accomplished without fastening the cloth to a printing board if care is taken that no wrinkles occur under the block. For the printing of large pieces, however, or when printing repeat patterns, the cloth should be tightly stretched across a printing board covered with table felt or heavy thicknesses of newspaper, as discussed in Chapter 4.

3. Kits are available similar to the one shown in Fig. 175, which contain the basic supplies and equipment for block printing.

Figs. 176 and 177 illustrate simple products which can be block printed by the beginner. The first is a half-drop over-all repeat monogram printed on a silk kerchief, while the second shows a border repeat block printed on a cotton luncheon cloth set.

Fig. 175. Kit for Block Printing (Courtesy, X-Acto-Cresent Products Co.)

Fig. 176. Half-Drop Over-All Repeat Monogram (Courtesy, American Crayon Co.)

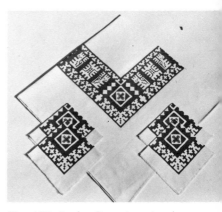

Fig. 177. Border Repeat on Luncheon Set (Courtesy, **American Home Magazine**)

CHAPTER 11

Linoleum Block Printing in Several Colors

Fig. 178. Two Color Place Mat (Courtesy, American Crayon Co.)

In planning for multicolor block printing the same principles applied to any of the techniques must be considered. Of primary importance is the choice of colors and the arrangement of the colors on the cloth. The color of the cloth itself cannot be ignored. Next in importance is the planning for the layout.

Types of Two Color Work

Fig. 178 illustrates a two color place mat in which neither of the two colors comes into direct contact with the other. The planning for this type of multicolor block print is simple; merely the space relationship has to be planned. Since outlines do not have to meet precisely, the drawings and the actual blocks do not have to be executed in perfect "register" to each other. (See Chapter 6 for a full discussion of register.)

The second type of two color print is shown in Fig. 179. The same block is used for both imprints, but two different colors are used, one overlapping the other. When used as a spot design on napkins, hand towels, etc., this technique is relatively simple. No special problem in registering more than one block presents itself. Fig. 180 shows a multicolor, over-all repeat pattern in which different colors have been utilized, but, once again, the various colors do not meet or overlap. A careful study of this repeat pattern will disclose that it *does follow* an established and regular repeat which was planned by the artist.

The print being made in Fig. 181 presents the most advanced and most difficult of the multicolor techniques. In this over-all repeat pattern, each area of the first color must "strike" at a predeter-

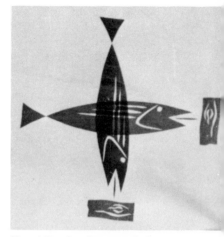
Fig. 179. Overlapping Color Prints, Same Block (Courtesy, American Crayon Co.)

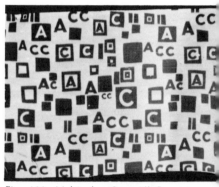
Fig. 180. Multicolor Over-All Repeat (Courtesy, American Crayon Co.)

Fig. 181. Registered, Over-All Repeat Pattern

83

Fig. 182. Register Jig

Fig. 183. Place Block in Jig

mined place and the second color must
overprint at precise locations. In planning this type of block print design,
some means has to be devised for cutting
each color block, whether two or ten, so
that in the final printing the colors will
appear where desired.

A Simple Register Device

Fig. 182 illustrates a simple device
for registering the sketches for tracing,
and the blocks, preparatory to cutting.
This "register jig" consists of a ply-
wood baseboard approximately 10 by 14
inches in size. On top of this board are
strips of wood of the same thickness as
unmounted battleship linoleum (usually,
one-fourth of an inch thick) forming an
inverted "L" section on the upper left.
A heavier piece of wood (held in the
hand in Fig. 182) is hinged to the back
so that it can be lowered into or raised
out of place, as desired. The edge of this
piece of wood, when lowered, is flush
with the top of the opening created by
the inverted "L" strippings. The total

84

thickness of this edge will equal that of *mounted* linoleum (usually three-quarters of an inch).

To use this jig for cutting the two blocks for the print in Fig. 181, the hinged section was lowered to accommodate a piece of mounted linoleum the size of the pattern. Fig. 183 illustrates the linoleum block being placed into the jig. The drawing containing both color areas is then tacked securely into place over the linoleum block, Fig. 184. The drawing is tacked to the jig, not the block. Using carbon paper and a pencil, the *first* color area is carefully traced onto the surface of the linoleum.

The block is then removed, and without disturbing the sketch, the second block is placed into the jig, Fig. 185. The *second* color area is now traced onto the second block with carbon paper and pencil. If the print were to contain more than two colors, each successive color block would be traced in this same manner. Each block now has the appropriate color tracing on it in precise relationship to the original sketch *and* to each other.

Fig. 184. Tack Drawing to Jig   Fig. 185. Insert Second Block in Jig

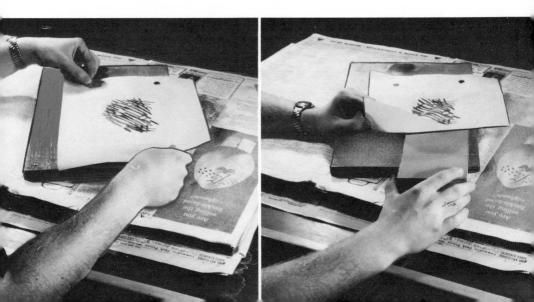

Cut the blocks according to previous instructions. Prepare the paint, mixing it thoroughly on a glass slab, Fig. 186, and strike test prints on pieces of paper. These test prints will aid the artist in determining whether certain areas should be cut deeper to prevent unwanted portions from printing.

It is assumed at this point in preparing for the multicolor print, that the design and repeat pattern have been decided upon. It is also assumed that the blocks have been cut in perfect register and that the test prints have proven satisfactory. It remains then, to accomplish the printing, which also has to be done "in register."

Making the Prints

For the home or school craftsman preparing a relatively short run of printed material, a small printing board can be arranged for printing in register. This type of board is shown in use in Fig. 187 in printing the first color of the over-all repeat. The board, of convenient size,

Fig. 186. Mix Ink Thoroughly on Slab

Fig. 187. Small Printing Board — Note Register Guides

is first padded with thick table felt or heavy newspaper padding as explained in Chapter 4. Strips of heavy twine or lacing are attached vertically across the board at the proper intervals to accommodate the width of the block. In this type of repeat, the strips serve as guides for the left- and right-hand edges of the block. Since the first color is a solid area imprint, the upper and lower dimensions of the block prove no problem. After the full surface attached to the board has been printed, the thumb tacks are removed from the cloth, the printed portion is slid out of the "register" under the strips, and a fresh area is moved into place. This is repeated until the entire length of the cloth is printed.

After the first color has dried, the second color is printed in the same manner. Here again, the edges of the first imprint serve as guides to the upper and lower dimensions of the block. If this is not the case, small chalk marks can be made on the strips to indicate register.

Fig. 188. Remove Ink from Non-Printing Areas

Fig. 189. Clean Block After Printing

Additional Hints

1. It may be necessary after each inking of the block to wipe away any excess ink or paint which appears on areas where not desired. This is readily accomplished by wrapping a small piece of cloth around the finger and carefully removing the unwanted paint, Fig. 188.

2. After the printing is complete, the block should be thoroughly cleaned with a mild solvent such as kerosene, Fig. 189. It is important to keep in mind that most textile paints are thermosetting, and will harden in air to almost irremov-

Fig. 190. Infra-Red Lamp Used for Heat-Setting

able hardness. Any scraping or abusive cleaning techniques after the paint has hardened will result in damage to the printing surface of the linoleum.

3. Various heat-setting techniques have been discussed in this book. Most textile paints require this for thorough "curing" and color fastness. Another convenient method entails the use of an inexpensive infa-red lamp, Fig. 190. The lamp is used in any lamp socket and can be held in position over the printed area for approximately three minutes. Hold the lamp about 12 inches from the printed surface.

CHAPTER 12

Other Types of Block Printing

Block printing in its earliest forms undoubtedly utilized the carved stone and, later on, the carved piece of wood. It is difficult to attempt to visualize how certain crafts originated, except by speculation. It appears logical that once man had discovered the use of dyes or coloring materials taken from metallic oxides and vegetable substances, he was not long in discovering the process of imprinting. Possibly his dye-covered hand proved to be the first "block print".

Some of the earliest recorded block prints are those produced from fine grained wood blocks. As civilized man learned the properties of wood, he discovered that end-grain was less subject to warping, and hence was perfectly suited to carving fine designs and patterns. Fine wood blocks are often used by artists today. They are produced by gluing small pieces of end-grain boxwood together. On this ultra-smooth surface, the design is painstakingly carved, Fig. 191. Carving wood is a

Fig. 191. End-Grain Boxwood Block

Fig. 192. Over-All Repeat—Pine Block

Fig. 193. Full-Drop Repeat — Interesting Texture

much more difficult technique than carving on linoleum, but finer, more detailed lines can be produced.

Contemporary Techniques

The modern artist, with his continued interest in the use of wood and wood grains for producing block prints, can sometimes achieve startling results by allowing the grain of the wood to form the core of the design. Fig. 192 illustrates an over-all repeat design produced with a rectangular block of soft wood, such as pine. The "U" shaped gouge was used to carve out random strips of the wood. The block was inked in the usual manner and printed in a rotated repeat pattern. (See Chapter 5.) In Fig. 193, the end of a strip of stock two inches square was cut at various locations with a back saw. This end was then inked and used to produce the full drop repeat shown.

90

In Fig. 194, wood was used as a printing material rather than a source of textural pattern. Odd shapes were cut from a one-half inch board with a coping saw and these pieces then used as printing blocks.

Variety Techniques

For the variety techniques of block printing which follow, it is suggested that a commercial grade of textile paint, such as *Prang* be used. The advantage in a commercial grade is that it has a greater viscosity and will adhere better to the various objects used for printing. In *preparing any* commercial block printing paint, the manufacturer's instructions should be followed carefully. Various *extendors* must be mixed in the proportions required, Fig. 195.

Fig. 196 shows a potato print. The potato is cut in half and a design is cut with a pen knife. This surface is then inked with the rubber roller and textile paint and imprinted in the repeat desired. The water in the potato prevents the paint from saturating the "block," hence it proves to be an excellent medium for this use.

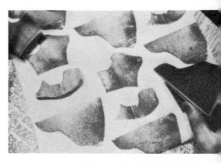

Fig. 194. Wood Forms Used for Direct Printing

Fig. 195. Mix Paint to Manufacturer's Directions

Fig. 196. Potato Print

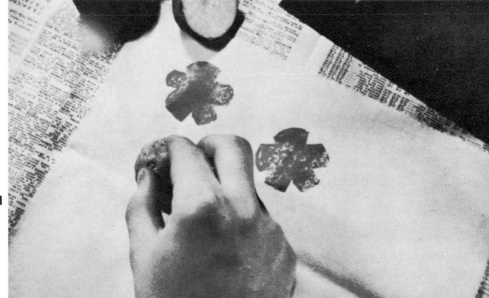

Fig. 197. Bottle Cork and Eraser Prints

Fig. 198. Bottle Cap Prints

Fig. 199. Rubber Strip Prints

Fig. 197 illustrates simple block prints made from bottle corks and erasers. The surface of the cork or the eraser is carved with a pen knife or razor blade to the desired pattern, then it is inked and imprinted. Certain of these small "blocks" can be inked by impressing them on the ink plate, in the manner of using a rubber stamp pad, and then imprinting them on the cloth.

Figs. 198 and 199 show but two samples of an unlimited source of original patterns. Various objects are merely adhered to a block of wood, inked, and then imprinted. In Fig. 198, soft drink bottle caps were attached to the block. In Fig. 199, strips of rubber bands were adhered with rubber cement. Various flat materials can be adhered to a block in this manner, such as the strip of burlap shown in Fig. 200, to produce unusual results. Even rubber cement itself can be spread *unevenly* on a block, allowed to dry, and then used for printing.

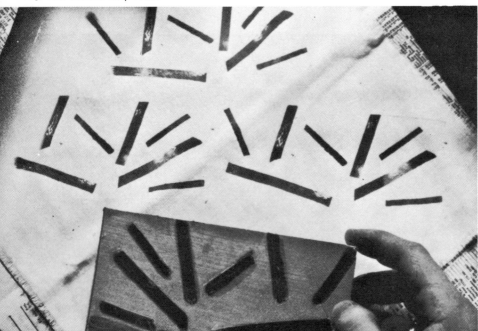

Fig. 200. Burlap Print

A variety of common objects, such as the potato masher shown in Fig. 201, can also be used for creating novel design results. The surface of the object is inked and then used as the "printing block." Machine gears, vegetable graters, and table forks of various sizes, are but a few of the objects which can be used in this technique. For designs which approach the naturalistic in shape and form, roots, large leaves, pieces of bark, and even blossoms of plants can have paint applied to them and then be used for imprinting.

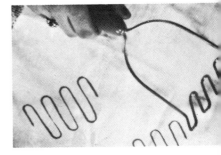

Fig. 201. Potato Masher Print

Additional References

Corbin, T. J., *Hand Block Printing on Fabrics.* London: Isaac Pitman, 1934.

Greenberg, Samuel, *Making Linoleum Cuts.* New York: Stephen Daye Press, 1947.

Kafka, Francis J., *Linoleum Block Printing.* Bloomington, Illinois: McKnight & McKnight Publishing Co., 1955. *(Dover reprint)*

CHAPTER 13

Free-Hand Painting

Very little assistance can be given with methods and techniques for freehand painting because, for the most part, they depend upon an ability to use a paint brush in the application of relatively original designs. Fig. 202 shows a table cloth decorated in the freehand style, resulting however, in a symmetric motif. On close examination, almost every freehand decoration will show minor variations in the line work even when a patttern is repeated.

Preparations for Painting

The first step in preparation for painting is the preparation of the pigment itself. Any one of those previously mentioned may be used, but the one chosen must be mixed to the proper consistency, and in the case of commercial preparations, according to the manufacturer's directions. Place a quantity of the pigment on a glass slab. Use a spatula to work in the proper extendors and mordants. All pigments for freehand painting must be of *thinner* consistency than for any of the other

Fig. 202. Freehand Decoration — Symmetrical Motif (Courtesy, American Crayon Co.)

techniques, Fig. 203. If the article being decorated will not be subjected to frequent laundering, ordinary artist tube color thinned with equal proportions of turpentine and strong vinegar may be used. The special mordant discussed in Chapter 2 may also be used by adding enough of it to the tube color to thin it to proper consistency.

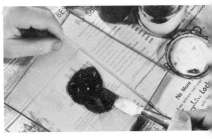

Fig. 203. Paint Is Thin

The cloth is first thoroughly laundered and ironed flat. It is best for most work to fasten the cloth tightly on a board with four or five layers of newspaper under the cloth. No special brushing technique is required. The brush should be charged with paint and then run across a piece of blotting paper to remove any excess. For simple, personalized designs, the artist works freehand on the cloth either following a sketch or working from his own imagination and creativeness. Occasionally, light pencil lines may be used as guide lines. However, these must be avoided when working with light colored pigments, or they may appear through the color. Fig. 204 illustrates the application of small, novelty designs to fabric for nursery curtains.

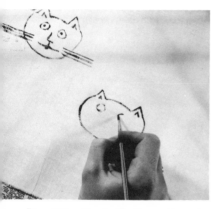

Fig. 204. Freehand Decoration for Nursery Curtains

Fig. 205. Laying Out Repeat Pattern

Repeat Patterns

Over-all repeat patterns are planned in the manner explained in Chapter 5. Working on a large sheet of blank newsprint, the artist roughly sketches in the

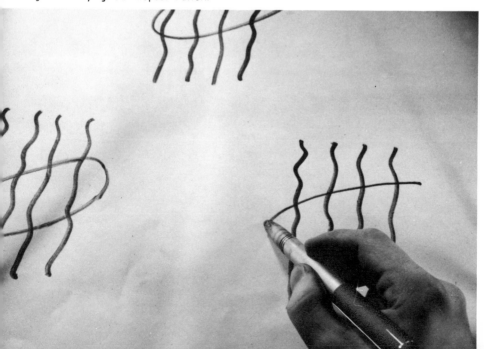

design motifs and the location of each repeat, Fig. 205. The measurements are transferred to the cloth. The general areas where the freehand painting is to be accomplished are marked off by applying small strips of pressure adhesive draftsman's tape, Fig. 206. The artist then proceeds to apply the color. Multicolor work presents no special problem. One color may be applied at a time, or the entire design can be finished in all required colors before moving on to the next repeat.

Spatter Techniques

A certain degree of rigidity and uniformity can be given to repeat motifs by utilizing the "spatter print" technique through a stencil, Fig. 207. A stencil previously used in the stenciling technique may be used for this variation. When placing the stencil on the cloth, *cover the exposed surface of the cloth with newspaper* for a distance of about 1½ feet on all sides of the stencil. Charge a discarded tooth-

Fig. 206. Laying Out Decoration Areas

Fig. 207. Spatter Print Stencil

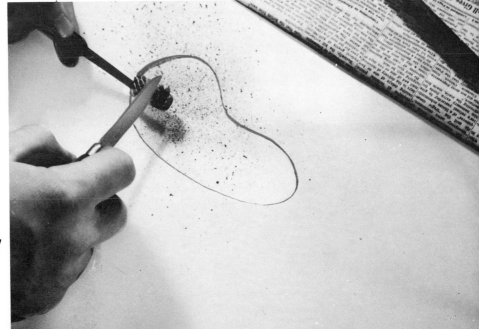

Fig. 208. Reverse Spatter Print

brush with fairly thin paint. Hold the brush about six inches from the stencil opening, and run the back of a knife blade across the bristles, *drawing the blade toward you*, as shown in Fig. 207, thus spattering paint through the stencil onto the cloth. No two painted areas will be exactly alike, although the outlines will be the same on all.

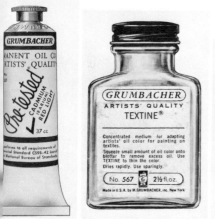

Fig. 209. Artist's Tube Color

Fig. 210. Washproof Compound (Courtesy, M. Grumbacher, Inc.)

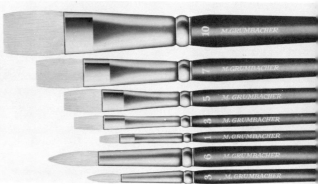

Fig. 211. Artist's Brushes (Courtesy, M. Grumbacher, Inc.)

A reverse stencil spatter technique can be accomplished by using the portion of the stencil which has been cut out (and which is normally discarded). Place this on the cloth, Fig. 208, and spatter print it in the same manner as before. The covered area will remain unpainted while the surrounding areas will be spattered, thus creating a "negative" imprint. Interesting results in this technique can be experienced by using large leaves and other flat objects as the stencils.

Colors

Interesting freehand designs can be accomplished on fabric by using ordinary artist's tube color, Fig. 209. In order to make these colors washproof, a commercial material such as *Textine*, Fig. 210, is added to the color. A high quality of tube color should be used, and the excess oil should be removed from the paint by squeezing a small amount of it onto a desk blotter. A good variety of sizes of brushes in rounds and flats is required for freehand work, Fig. 211.

Among the many commercially available paints made especially for fabric painting are *Decora* and *Flo-Pacque*. *Decora*, Fig. 212, is a liquid of almost watery consistency which must be applied very carefully and very lightly to prevent smudging. The fibers of the cloth readily absorb the paint.

Flo-Paque, Fig. 213, is one of the most versatile of paints. It has the consistency of milk or very light syrup and brushes very well. It can be used for

Fig. 212. Fabric Painting Set (Courtesy, F. Weber Co.)

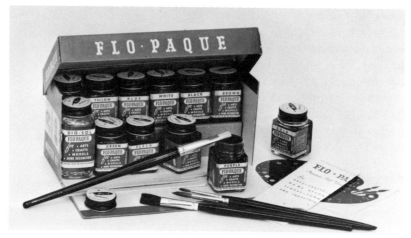

Fig. 213. Versatile Paint Set (Courtesy, Floquil Products, Inc.)

Fig. 214. Pieces Decorated Freehand (Courtesy, Floquil Products, Inc.)

the decoration of many materials besides fabrics and is available in a wide range of colors, including the metallics. It is opaque and will decorate the *surface* of the fabric rather than being absorbed too deeply into the fibers. It has the great virtue of being thermosetting; therefore, the colors can be made washproof by the application of heat as in previously discussed paints. Figs. 214 and 215 illustrate some articles decorated with *Flo-Paque*.

Additional References

Cox, Doris, and Barbara Warren Weismann, *Creative Hands*. New York: John Wiley & Sons, Inc., 1945.

Design Technics. Columbus, Ohio: Design Publishing Co., n/d.

Flam, David, *1001 Designs For Hand Decorating*. New York: Homecrafts, 1950.

Hallen, Julienne, *300 Projects For Hand Decorating*. New York: Homecrafts, 1950.

Moore, Edwena B., *Textile Painting*. San Diego: The Adept Litho Arts, 1949.

Now You Can Do It Yourself. Sandusky, Ohio: The American Crayon Co., n/d.

Paint It Yourself. West End, New Jersey:
CVH Laboratories Co., 1950.

Yates, Raymond F., *The Hobby Book of Stenciling and Brush-Stroke Painting*. New
York: McGraw-Hill Book Co., 1951.

Fig. 215. Freehand Decoration (Courtesy, Floquil Products, Inc.)

Fig. 216. Screen Frame and Colors

Fig. 217. Stencil Attached to Silk

Fig. 218. Pour Paint Into Well

Silk Screen Printing

Silk screen printing is a stenciling technique — the paint is applied to the finished product *through* a cut out stencil which *resists* the application of paint to certain areas. As discussed in Chapter 2, the great limitation of the pure stencil technique has always been the necessity for using "bridges" or "ties" to hold the various components of the design together. The silk screen is man's solution to this problem.

A mesh fabric is stretched very tightly across a heavy wood frame, Fig. 216. The cut out stencil of the required design is attached securely to the underside of this stretched fabric, Fig. 217. Special paint is poured into the "well" or recessed side of the stretched frame, Fig. 218. A squeegee, Fig. 219, which is a heavy rubber blade mounted in a sturdy wooden handle, is used to force the paint through the mesh of the fabric onto the surface to be printed, Fig. 220. The inherent virtue of this tightly

Fig. 219. Squeegee

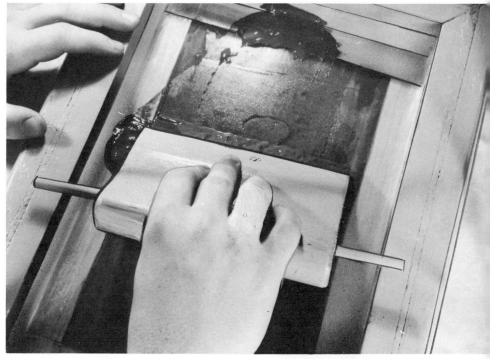

Fig. 220. Force Paint Through Stencil

stretched, mesh fabric is that the paint will not run through the mesh of its own accord, but it can be forced through mechanically. When the screen frame is lifted away from the surface of the cloth being printed, the neatly printed pattern is disclosed, Fig. 221.

Fig. 222 shows a classic example of the complexity in design which this process is capable of reproducing. Figs. 223, 224, and 225 illustrate a few outstanding modern prints produced by the silk

Fig. 221. Printed Design

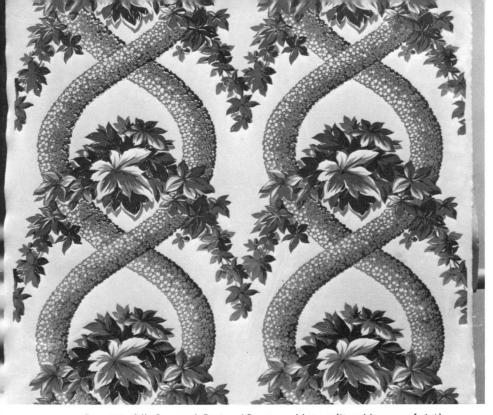

Fig. 222. Silk Screened Design (Courtesy, Metropolitan Museum of Art)
Fig. 223. Screened Luncheon Set (Courtesy, American Crayon Co.)

Fig. 224. Screened Fabrics (Courtesy, American Crayon Co.)
Fig. 225. Screened Drapery Fabrics (Courtesy, American Crayon Co.)

Fig. 226. Professional Workers (Courtesy, American Crayon Co.)

Fig. 227. Materials and Equipment

screen process. Fig. 226 depicts screen printing of textile material in a professional studio. It will be noted that the fabric is attached to a large printing table. The screen is also of a size which requires two persons to manipulate it. The basic process remains the same, however.

Supplies and Equipment Needed

It is suggested that the craftsman procure just the very essential items to begin a simple project in screen printing. Shown in Fig. 227 are: a stretched frame, a squeegee, a supply of special paint, and a cut out paper stencil. In addition to this — cleaning materials, a cutting tool for cutting the stencil, and, of course, the fabric to be printed — will be needed. The squeegee is best purchased ready-made. These are sold by the inch and should be approximately

106

one inch shorter than the width of the inside of the frame. For short runs, where a great deal of wear on the squeegee *will not take place,* a thoroughly smooth strip of hardwood (such as birch or maple), or even an ordinary window cleaning squeegee, may be used as substitutes for the silk screen squeegee, Fig. 228. The mesh fabric is usually referred to by "the trade" as silk, regardless of the material component. It is available in cotton organdy, taffeta, nylon, and dacron, with the cottons being the least expensive. These fabrics are graded by mesh count. A practical grade for the beginner is No. 12XX. The *finer* the mesh the lighter will be the deposit of paint. A heavier deposit of paint is usually required when printing on textiles because the fibers absorb the paint.

Fig. 228. Squeegee Substitutes

Preparing the Printing Frame

The printing frame may be purchased, assembled or unassembled, and either prestretched or not stretched. Or, it may be constructed at home or in school at very low cost. If it is to be homemade, certain assembling tools and supplies will be needed. Fig. 229 shows the author cutting strips of $1\frac{1}{2}''$ x $1\frac{1}{2}''$ "square stock" of pine with a back saw. A convenient sized frame for the beginner is one that has inside or "well" dimensions of approximately 10″ x 14″.

Fig. 229. Cutting Strips for Frame

Fig. 230 shows the four pieces of stock being assembled. Any type joint may be used by those who are familiar with woodworking joinery. The *butt* joint illustrated is as practical as any for this purpose. The joints need not be glued, and ordinary nails may be used for connecting. It is important, however,

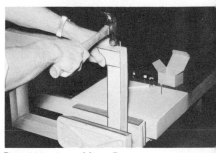
Fig. 230. Assembling Frame

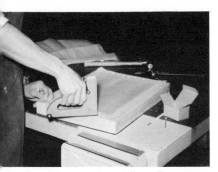

Fig. 231. Attaching Silk to Frame

Fig. 232. Stapling Gun (Courtesy, Arrow Fastener Co.)

Fig. 233. Sealing Inside Edges

that the pieces be of the exact size so that a perfectly square frame results. It is also important when assembling the pieces that the flat surfaces are flush with each other so that the finished frame will lie flat.

Next, the silk is attached to one side of the frame, Fig. 231. This may be done with small carpet tacks or by using a stapling gun, Fig. 232. If tacks are used, aluminum or copper tacks are preferred because they do not rust. To attach the silk, cut a piece to the exact dimensions of the outside of the frame. Staple or tack *one* long side flush with the edge of the frame and with the strands in the silk mesh running perfectly parallel to the edge of the frame. Pull the silk taut while attaching it. Next, attach one of the adjoining sides, being sure again that the weave of the material runs parallel to the edge of the frame. Next, attach the opposite *long* side, pulling the silk quite tightly to assure that no loose areas or "sags" appear. Finally, attach the last edge, tightening up *all* looseness.

Next, the screen is washed in a sink under a fast jet of water. This removes

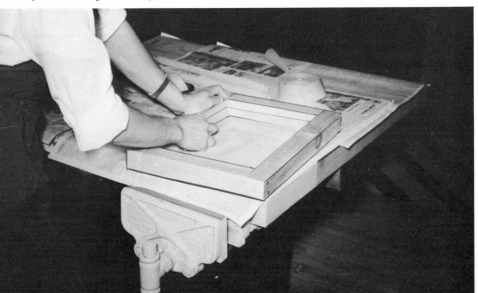

any filler or sizing which may have been used in the manufacturing of the silk and also gives the stretched silk a final tightening. It should have the "feel" of a drumhead at this point. Without waiting for the frame to dry, strips of gummed paper tape are attached to all four inside edges, Fig. 233. The tape strips are folded in the center lengthwise and placed so that one half is attached to the silk and the other half attached to the wood of the frame. Small pieces of the tape must also be attached to the inside corners to seal the joint lines. If any difficulty is encountered in obtaining perfect adhesion of the gummed tape, a little liquid glue may be added to the water used for moistening the tape.

Gummed tape is then attached to the outside surface of the screen, Fig. 234, to cover the tacks or staples and to protect the raw edges of the piece of silk. Allow the frame to dry completely. If the screen has been properly stretched, it will be *perfectly* tight and free from any sagging when it has dried.

After drying, all of the paper surfaces are given a coating of shellac, Fig. 235. Shellac is used because the only efficient

Fig. 234. Covering Tacks or Staples

Fig. 235. Shellacking Paper Surfaces

solvent for it is wood alcohol. Since wood alcohol will not be used either in printing or in cleaning the frame later on, the shellac coating will remain intact. When the shellac has dried, the frame is ready for use.

Fig. 236 illustrates a complete, packaged silk screen printing kit which is available for the artist or craftsman who does not wish to make or improvise a frame.

The Technique

Use one of the methods of design development outlined in Chapters 3, 4, and 6, to obtain a design. It is suggested that a simple "spot" design in one color be used for the first experiment. Following the instructions given in Chapter 2, cut the design out of a piece of waxed stencil board or good quality bond paper with a stencil knife or a razor blade, Fig. 237. Waxed stencil board, which is available commercially, has the advantage of being transparent enough to trace a design directly through the stencil board.

When the stencil has been cut, attach it to the screen frame using pressure

Fig. 236. Silk Screen Printing Kit (Courtesy, Naz-Dar Co.)

Fig. 237. Cut Design With Stencil Knife

sensitive adhesive tape or draftsman's tape, Fig. 217. Be sure that the edges of the stencil which rest on the screen frame are completely sealed with tape. Any open areas of the silk mesh which have not been covered by the stencil board also have to be sealed. Remember that any open area on the surface of the silk will ultimately have paint forced through it.

Special textile paints (discussed more fully in Chapter 17) must be used if the article printed is intended to be laundered or dry cleaned. Since larger quantities of these paints are needed for the screen process method than are needed in other methods of printing, it is advisable to purchase these already prepared. Pour a sizeable quantity (several heaping tablespoonfuls) into the "well" of the printing frame, Fig. 218. Place the "charged" frame on a sheet of newspaper and make a print using the squeegee to force the paint through the stencil, Fig. 220. Examine the print to make sure the screen is reproducing properly. This first printing will also adhere the waxed stencil firmly to the silk so that repeated imprints may be made.

If the print is satisfactory, place the frame over the tightly stretched cloth to be printed, and print the impression. Pre-arranged locations for the imprints can be managed with tape registers as explained in Chapter 3. Some of the stencils used in Chapters 2, 3, and 4 can be re-used for silk screen printing. When printing more complicated designs, especially those having separate component parts which have *not* been *bridged* or *tied* together, the small

Fig. 238. Glue Pieces to Screen

Fig. 239. Printed Design

pieces may be adhered directly to the screen with thin glue, Fig. 238. The large, open area is cut out of a full sheet of stencil board and mounted on the screen with tape, as previously explained. The resulting print is shown in Fig. 239.

For Longer Runs

The paper stencil method outlined above is a practical method for "short runs" of not more than 30 or 40 imprints. Beyond this, the stencil usually becomes saturated with the paint and does not continue to adhere thoroughly to the silk. However, this number of imprints frequently proves sufficient, especially for the beginner. If a larger "run" is required, and the paper stencil is utilized, the *shellac stencil* is recommended.

Coat a sheet of high quality bond paper or sturdy wrapping paper with shellac, brushing it on evenly, Fig. 240.

Fig. 240. Shellac Bond Paper

Allow the sheet to dry thoroughly (several hours at least) in a hanging position. Excess shellac will then run to the lower edge, which can be trimmed off with scissors.

Cut the stencil in the same manner as the waxed board stencil is cut. To adhere it to the screen, place it beneath the silk on the frame, and run a warm iron back and forth across the surface of the silk, Fig. 241. The heat will cause the shellac to become tacky, and this tackiness will adhere it to the silk. The edges of the stencil are taped to the screeen in the same manner as before.

Fig. 241. Adhere With Warm Iron

After the printing is complete, the screen frame and squeegee are cleaned as described in Chapter 15. The waxed board stencil can be merely pulled free of the frame. The shellac stencil, however, will have to be dissolved free with wood alcohol. Keeping paper stencils for future use is *not* recommended. Both the wax and the shellac usually lose their effectiveness in adhering to the silk after they have been exposed to the printing paint.

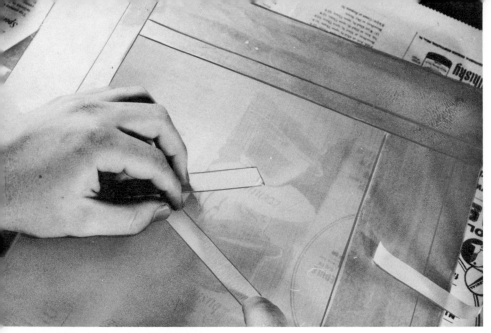

Fig. 242. Designing With Pressure Adhesive Tape

Fig. 243. Printed Design

Additional Hints

Some very interesting abstract patterns may be created through the use of simple materials and a little originality. The following are but a few examples.

1. Pieces of pressure adhesive tape can be arranged on the surface of the silk, Fig. 242. A piece of stencil board with an irregularly shaped opening cut through it is then mounted on the frame. The resulting print is shown in Fig. 243.

2. Loose-leaf reinforcement patches can be attached to the screen in the same manner, Fig. 244. After the cut-out stencil board (technically called a frisquet) has been attached, an original print is obtained, Fig. 245.

3. Fresh garden leaves and petals of flowers can be carefully attached

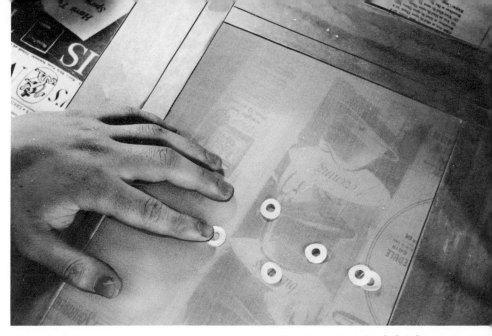

Fig. 244. Loose-Leaf Reinforcements
Offer Design Possibilities

to the screen with thin glue and printed in the same manner.

4. Many other conventional shapes, such as those found in gift package seals (bells, pumpkins, stars, etc.), can be utilized in the same manner as the loose-leaf reinforcements.

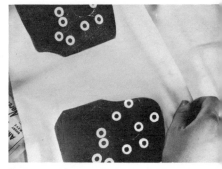

Fig. 245. Abstract Print

CHAPTER 15

Silk Screening Repeat Patterns

As stencil patterns become more involved, such as the one the artist is developing in Fig. 246, it becomes increasingly difficult to mount the *entire* stencil on the screen. To overcome this difficulty, a special stencil material known as *lacquer film* was invented. It is available under many trade names such as *Nu-Film, Pro-Film*, etc. It consists of a thin sheet of lacquer attached to a slightly oiled backing paper. The

Fig. 246. Fine-Line Design

sheet is highly transparent and is available in various colors: amber; green, for eye-ease; and blue, for transmitting colors better. It is handled in much the same way as the paper board with one important exception: *only the lacquer* is cut through with the stencil cutting knife, while the paper backing remains uncut. Following the cutting process, the lacquer in the *open areas* in the stencil (those areas which will print on the finished article) is removed. When the lacquer is adhered to the silk on the frame, the paper backing is carefully peeled away, thus leaving all of the component parts of the stencil adhered in place on the silk. This chapter will discuss printing a repeat pattern on cloth with the lacquer stencil method.

Materials Needed

In addition to those already listed in the previous chapter, the following are required for lacquer stencil screening:

Lacquer film. Sold by the running yard. May be purchased in quarter and half yards.

Adhering liquid. A specially prepared lacquer thinner which adheres the lacquer film to the silk.

Blockout liquid. Either a heavy, dense lacquer, or a thick water soluble material, used for painting those areas on the silk which the lacquer film stencil has not covered.

Lacquer thinner. Ordinary commercial grade, used for dissolving the stencil from the screen when it is no longer needed.

Brush. For applying the blockout liquid. A brush used for lacquer should never be used for any other substance. A one-half inch, inexpensive paint brush will do.

Stencil knife. Traditionally a smaller, narrower blade is used for cutting lacquer film than for cutting paper stencils. However, some artists use the same knife.

In planning a repeat print in silk screen, the same preliminary outlining and computing must be accomplished, as in any type of repeat print. This is explained fully in Chapter 5. The design may be developed in any manner previously described (Chapters 3, 4, and 6). As shown in Fig. 246, the artist has developed a freehand abstract design to be used as a border repeat suitable for tablecloths, draperies, and other articles. Since this design will have to be "connected" as each pattern is repeated to give the continuous effect desired, the left end of the pattern will have to blend satisfactorily into the right end of the pattern on the drawing.

Procedure

After the drawing is complete in every detail, mount it with tape on a stiff piece of bristol board. Cut a piece of lacquer film approximately the size of the exposed *silk* on the printing frame to be used. Using tape again, mount this sheet of lacquer film (shiny, or lacquer side up) over the drawing so that the drawing is in the approximate center of the piece of film.

With the stencil knife, very carefully cut through the lacquer coating, but *not* through the paper backing. The knife must have an extremely keen edge so that a neat, precise cut is obtained.

Fig. 247. Begin Peeling With Knife Point

Ragged cuts will result in ragged edges on the final print. Where two lines meet each other and terminate, it is advisable to prolong each cut about one-eighth of an inch so that a clean-cut corner results. When the cutting is complete, strip away all of the *open* areas of the stencil. Use the point of the knife to start the peeling, and the fingers to complete the process, Fig. 247.

Place the completed stencil, lacquer side *up,* on several thicknesses of newspaper. Place the clean screen frame over the stencil in the usual *printing* position. Make sure that the design is centered properly under the silk and is in proper alignment with the edges of the frame.

Fig. 248. Adhere Small Area at One Time

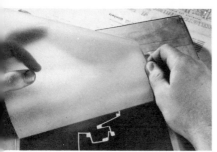

Fig. 249. Remove Backing Sheet

Pour a small quantity of *adhering liquid* into a shallow dish. The adhering process is best accomplished by using two small pieces of rag, one in each hand. Moisten one rag and apply it carefully to a small area of the silk. With the dry rag, immediately rub this moistened area briskly to dry it and adhere the lacquer, Fig. 248. If the film is properly adhered, that area will darken in appearance. If it has not adhered, it must be treated again. The artist must be very cautious in using the adhering liquid to insure that too much is not applied. The liquid actually dissolves the lacquer, so that it *is* possible to completely dissolve the stencil.

When the entire stencil has been adhered, turn the frame over and allow about ten minutes for drying. When dry, separate a corner of the lacquer film from the paper backing with the fingernail and carefully peel away the entire backing sheet, Fig. 249. If perfect

120

adhesion has taken place, *no portion* of the film will remain attached to the paper backing.

With the paint brush, carefully apply a small amount of *blockout liquid* to any open areas on the silk surrounding the edge of the stencil. Then apply four strips of pressure adhesive tape so that they cover the edges of the stencil, Fig. 250.

The cloth to be printed must be thoroughly washed and pressed flat. Tack it securely and tightly to a board which has been previously covered with felt or thick newspapers, Fig. 251. Compute the locations on the cloth where the imprints are to be made, using the instructions in Chapter 5. Mark these locations on the cloth with tape, thread, or in some other

Fig. 250. Cover Edges With Tape

Fig. 251. Secure Stretched Cloth to Printing Board

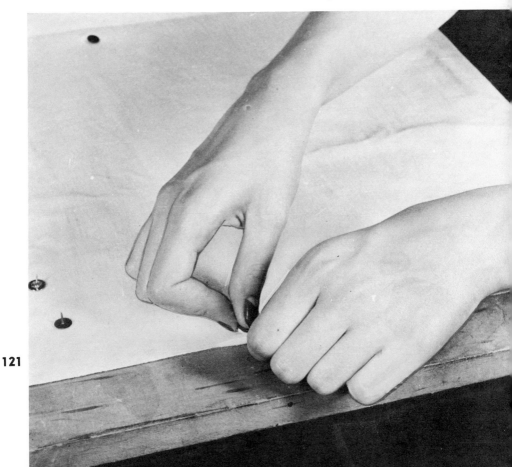

manner, Fig. 252. Proper *register* of the imprints cannot *possibly* be overemphasized. Figs. 253 and 254 illustrate the painstaking care and complicated registry devices used in studio printing of over-all repeat patterns. Nothing looks less professional than a repeat pattern in which the design areas do not fit against each other.

Make a trial print (or several of them) on a sheet of newspaper, Fig. 255. When satisfied with the trial prints, remove the newspaper and place the freshly laundered cloth to be decorated in the printing position. Print the entire strip, Fig. 256. When the screen is placed on top of a print just made, a slipsheet of newspaper should be placed over the freshly wet print, as explained in Chapter 4. Fig. 257 shows the com-

Fig. 252. Mark Cloth for Impressions

Fig. 253. Note Register Devices (Courtesy, Department of Art, Skidmore College)

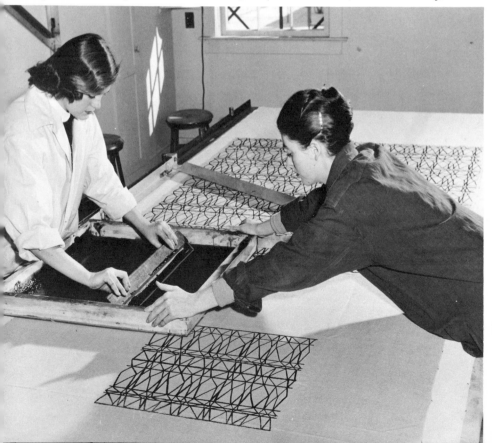

Fig. 254. Note Register Pin in Foreground (Courtesy, Department of Art, Skidmore College)

pleted print. When the printing has dried completely (overnight drying is recommended), the printed area should be treated according to the manufacturer's directions. This usually includes heat-setting with an iron for about three minutes, and thorough laundering in lukewarm water and a mild soap.

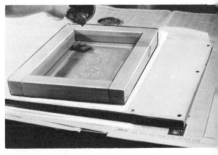

Fig. 255. Take Trial Print on Paper

Fig. 256. Print the Cloth

Fig. 257. Completed Print

123

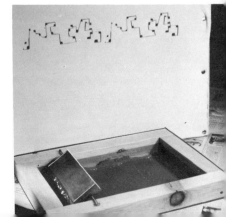

Preserving the Screen

If the screen is to be used for later prints with the same stencil, the excess paint is removed from the well of the screen by scooping it out with a piece of cardboard, Fig. 258. The entire screen is then thoroughly cleaned of all traces of paint, using a kerosene soaked cloth, Fig. 259. Both sides of the screen are cleaned, but care must be taken when working on the underside that the stencil is not damaged. The squeegee is thoroughly cleaned with kerosene. This cleaning should take place immediately after the printing is finished. Most textile paints, when allowed to dry on the screen, cannot be removed later without damage to the stencil, the silk, or both.

Fig. 258. Scoop Out Excess Paint

Fig. 259. Use Kerosene to Clean Screen of Paint

The lacquer film stencil cannot be *removed* from the screen for re-use. The only method of removing it is to completely dissolve it from the silk. If this is carefully done, and the silk thoroughly cleaned, the frame can be used for a new stencil without re-stretching it. To remove the stencil, place the frame in the printing position over a thick stack of newspaper. Pour a liberal quantity of lacquer thinner into the well. Allow it to soak for about five minutes and rub it vigorously with a clean rag, Fig. 260. Carefully lift the screen, allowing as much of the lacquer stencil as possible to adhere to the newspaper, Fig. 261. Repeat this as often as necessary. Use clean newspaper each time to remove all of the lacquer. Give the silk a final

Fig. 260. Use Lacquer Thinner to Soften Stencil

Fig. 261. Blot the Screen Onto Newspaper

Fig. 262. Professionally-Printed Over-All Repeat (Courtesy American Crayon Co.)

washing with more lacquer thinner and clean rags. When completely clean and free of any traces of lacquer, it is ready to have another stencil adhered to it. Textile paints sometimes "dye" the original open areas of the silk in the color which was used for printing. This does not matter. The artist must learn to distinguish between this and actual clogging of the mesh caused by lacquer or dry printing paint. Such clogging will not allow free flow of paint on future jobs.

Fig. 262 shows a professionally-printed over-all repeat of a much more complex nature than the samples shown in this chapter. It involves the use of more than one color, which the next chapter will discuss, and points out very graphically the importance of carefully-planned and accurately-executed registry.

CHAPTER 16

Silk Screen Printing

A silk screen technique which is used frequently where fine line work is desired and where a free-brushed appearance will enhance the print is the technique known as tusche-glue. Tusche,

Fig. 263. Sketch With Freehand Technique

also known as lithographer's wax, is a dense mixture of wax, oils, water, and lamp black. In its liquid state it can be readily thinned or dissolved with water. When it becomes hard and only the waxes remain, it is necessary to use kerosene or benzine to dissolve it.

Artists discovered that because of the nature of this substance (used for many years by lithographers) a silk screen stencil could be made by painting directly on the silk itself, offering greater freedom to the creative hand, and eliminating the use of a separately cut stencil. A sketch is made using a freehand technique, Fig. 263. The drawing is carefully placed on a drawing board, Fig. 264. The screen frame is lowered in the printing position over the sketch, so that it is visible through the silk, Fig. 265. Several small pieces of cardboard are inserted under the frame to raise the silk *slightly* above the sketch. Liquid tusche is then carefully brushed onto the silk, filling in the areas of the design, Fig. 266.

Fig. 265. Lower Frame Over Sketch

Fig. 266. Brush Tusche Into Design Areas

Fig. 267. Arrange Tracings of Design Elements

After the tusche has dried, ordinary animal glue is spread over the entire screen, using a square of heavy cardboard as a squeegee. Because the solvent of glue is water, it will not adhere to the hardened tusche, but only to the silk. When the glue has dried, the tusche is washed out of the silk with kerosene or benzine. Since these solvents will not dissolve hardened glue, the final result is an *open stencil* where tusche had originally been painted.

In abbreviated form, this is the process of tusche-glue stencil making. Its success depends upon the use of two liquid substances, both of which dry hard, and neither of which dissolves in the solvent for the other. Kerosene or benzine will dissolve the hardened tusche. Only water will dissolve the hardened glue. This chapter will discuss the use of the tusche-glue method in silk screen printing on fabrics in several colors.

Creating the Design

Correct register is even more important when printing in several colors because the design imprint must be accurately registered, as well as the various colors. The artist prepares the various component parts of the design, each on a separate sheet of translucent tracing paper. He places these one above the other and moves them about until he gets the combination he wants, Fig. 267. He then decides on the colors for each part of the design. He arranges the several drawings one above the other in the location decided upon. The drawing for the *first* color is placed on top, the second color is placed below it, and so on. It is both customary and advisable to print the lightest color first and the darkest color last. He then fastens these drawings down to a board.

Preparing the Stencils

Place the clean printing frame in the printing position so that the silk rests flat against the top drawing. With a soft pencil, trace the design directly onto the silk, Fig. 268.

Fig. 268. Trace Design Onto Silk

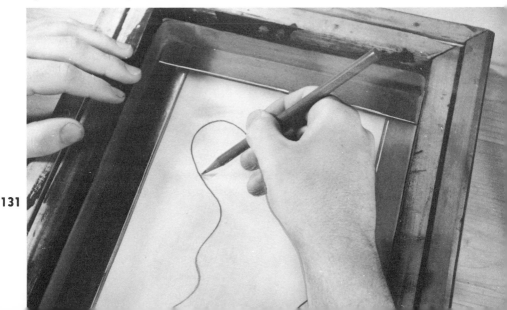

Fig. 269. Brush Tusche Into Design Area

Fig. 270. Cover Entire Screen With Glue

Fig. 271. Remove Tusche

Prop the frame up slightly by placing small squares of cardboard under each corner of the frame. Pour a little liquid tusche into a dish. With an artist's brush (preferably a round one), paint tusche over the entire design area, Fig. 269. Allow the tusche to air dry thoroughly.

When dry, pour a quantity of liquid animal glue into the well of the screen, and with a square of cardboard as a squeegee, spread the glue evenly back and forth over the entire silk area, Fig. 270. Do not be alarmed if the water in the glue causes the silk to sag. In drying, it will tighten again. When the glue has dried completely (it may take several hours), scrub every trace of tusche from the silk with a rag soaked in kerosene or benzine, Fig. 271. Stubborn spots of the tusche, particularly where the glue has become overly hard, can be removed by scraping very carefully with the fingernail, Fig. 272.

132

Invert the frame and seal the edges of the glue line with strips of tape, Fig. 273. It will be noticed on this illustration that a clear, open stencil has resulted.

Planning the Layout

If the preparatory planning for the proper register of the imprints has not previously been done, it should be done carefully at this time. One method of obtaining the proper locations for the imprints directly on the cloth is the one explained in Chapter 3. A series of prints or tracings of the design are made, and these are arranged on the cloth. When the arrangement is satisfactory, the screen is placed over each paper pattern, and the location of the screen frame is marked with small strips of tape. The cloth should be tightly fastened to a printing board, as in previous techniques, and should be free from creases.

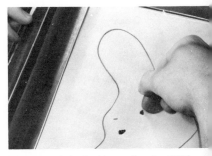

Fig. 272. Lift Stubborn Specks With Fingernail

Fig. 273. Seal Edges of Glue With Tape

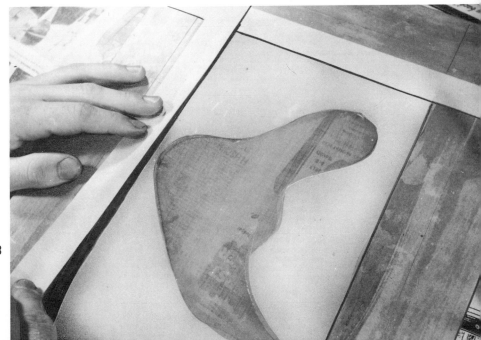

Fig. 274. Print in Desired Locations

Fig. 275. Clean Screen and Squeegee

Fig. 276. Remove Glue With Hot Running Water

Printing

Place the printing frame on a stack of newspapers. Pour in the paint and make several test runs on the paper.

When the design is printing properly, imprint the cloth in this *first* color in each location required, Fig. 274.

When the first printing is complete, clean the screen and squeegee with kerosene as before, Fig. 275. If the same frame is to be used for printing the second color, the glue will have to be removed. This is done by scrubbing the

134

silk carefully with a small hand brush under running hot water, Fig. 276.

When the screen is completely free of all glue, dry it, and proceed to trace, tusche in, glue coat, and remove tusche, as before. Proceed with all steps for the second color imprinting that were outlined for the first. The same procedure is followed for each successive color. Fig. 277 shows the finished print.

Other Applications

A variation in the tusche method is the use of a glass-marking grease pencil, Fig. 278, or a stick of solid tusche (commonly known as lithographer's crayon), Fig. 279, instead of a brush for applying liquid tusche. These substances wash out in the same manner, and their use en-

Fig. 277. Finished Print

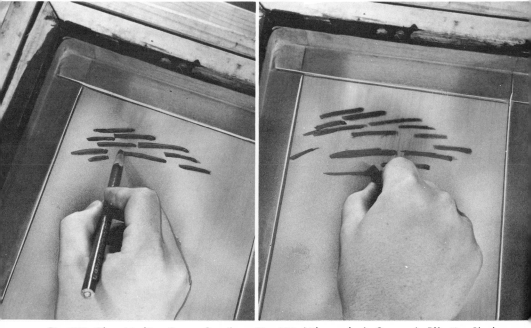

Fig. 278. Glass Marking Grease Pencil May Be Used

Fig. 279. Lithographer's Crayon Is Effective Block-Out

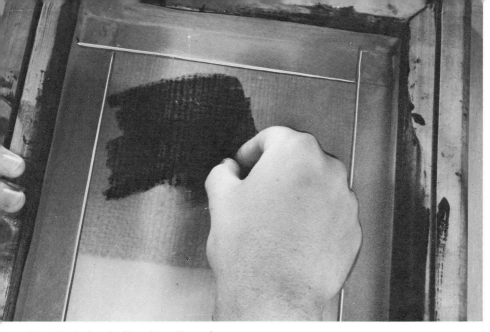

Fig. 280. Burlap Backing Gives Unusual Texture

Fig. 281. Interesting Tusche Screen (Courtesy, Department of Art, Skidmore College

ables the artist to develop interesting "stroke" patterns. Placing a piece of burlap or some other heavily textured material under the silk and rubbing the lithographer's crayon over the area, will likewise create unusual patterns, Fig. 280.

Fig. 281 shows an interesting tusche screen being prepared by an artist. Fig. 282 illustrates again the care which is taken to assure proper register. It will

be noted that the edge of the printing board has a strip of angle iron clamped to it. The frame is placed firmly against this guide as each successive imprint is made.

Figs. 283 and 284 are illustrations of several fine drapery materials screened with the soft flowing tusche-glue method.

Fig. 284. Unusual Drapery Material — Tusche Method Used (Courtesy, American Crayon Co.)

CHAPTER 17

Added Suggestions in Silk Screen

Silk Screen Pigments

One ingredient of any pigment, whether it is intended for use on paper, wood, glass, textiles, or some other printing surface, is the *vehicle*. This is a liquid, usually a petroleum product of some kind, into which color pigments can be mixed easily. Secondly, there is the *color* substance itself. This coloring material is not different from that used in any paint, except that it is very finely ground to permit passage through the mesh of the silk. Finally, various oils in the form of either *retarders* (to slow down drying time) or *driers* (to speed up drying time) are added to the mixture. Sometimes *fillers* are added. These are bulky substances of clay, grain flours, and other materials which tend to thicken and give body to the paint.

Several additional characteristics must mark screen pigments used for printing textiles: these pigments must contain permanent colors, and the pigment itself must permeate the fibers of the cloth to assure colorfastness in laundering and dry-cleaning.

Most of the older type, conventional textile paints contain special chemicals known as *mordants*. These act on the dyes to impart colorfastness to them and to assure full depth of color. With the development of synthetic pigments and vehicles, many of the newer textile paints are *thermosetting*. In other words they dry, set, and reach full permanence when heated. Just about any brand of textile paint manufactured by a reputable firm will meet the aforementioned requirements.

Special Pigments

Oil base. Most textile paints are classified as oil base paints; a petroleum derivative forms the vehicle. These paints are thinned with mineral spirits or with special *reducers* which are supplied by the manufacturer.

Water base. As the name implies, these pigments use water as a vehicle. They are durable and color fast after proper heat-setting but seem to lack the brightness and sparkle of oil base paints. They have the decided advantage of ease in cleaning the tools and equipment soiled in their use.

*Fast drying.** Certain pigments, particularly the lacquer base variety, used

---

* Lacquer base textile paints cannot be used when a lacquer film has been used for the stencil. The paint would eventually dissolve the stencil from the screen. Special, lacquer-proof film is available for this paint. The lacquer-proof film also requires a special adherent.

for some textile printing have the advantage of extremely rapid drying. This characteristic enables the finished articles to be stacked prior to heat-setting. However, the paint will also dry very rapidly on the equipment, especially the screen.

Da-Glo and Phosphorescent. Both of these novelty type paints are available for silk screen on textiles. Da-Glo gives the appearance of actually being illuminated because of its unusually high reflective value, while phosphorescent paints chemically absorb and store light which causes them to glow in the dark or under ultra-violet light (black light). These paints are frequently used for dramatic and theatrical affects.

Non-Curing. This is a special textile paint which does *not* require heat-setting prior to laundering and dry-cleaning. *Tex-Lac*, manufactured by the Colonial Process Supply Co., is one such product which gives the added advantage of very rapid surface drying.

Homemade Varieties. Completely satisfactory homemade pigments for silk screening present many difficulties, therefore they are not generally recommended. Because of the necessity for having very finely ground pigments which will penetrate the silk mesh, common paints are not advised. Printer's ink, oil base paint, and the white-of-egg, water-base paint — formulas for which are given in Chapter 3 — sometimes prove satisfactory. Usually, because of the larger working quantities of silk screen paint required, compared to other techniques, it proves just as economical for the artist to purchase the paint ready made.

General Cleanliness

Cleanliness in all areas of textile decoration is an important subject for the artist. Since almost all of the dyes, paints, and pigments used are, by their very nature, intended to permanently stain or color textile fibers, careless and accidental paint marks can easily ruin many hours of tedious work. Care and cleanliness is of even greater importance in silk screen because the fabric *used* for the stencil becomes saturated with paint during the printing operation. If this is not properly cleaned after use, especially in the case of the thermosetting variety of paints, it becomes virtually impossible to ever clean the screen for re-use. Paint which has been permitted to "cake" on the squeegee can also cause irreparable damage to this piece of equipment.

If it is absolutely necessary to suspend the printing operation for more than a few minutes *prior to the final cleaning* of the screen, a good technique is to place the screen in the printing position over a stack of flat newspapers. Place a clean piece of cloth directly onto the silk so that it fits flat and snugly. Moisten this cloth with mineral spirits or kerosene. This will prevent the paint from hardening on the screen. All traces of this solvent have to be carefully removed before printing can be resumed.

It must be remembered that even if the stencil is to be removed and the entire screen cleaned for the remounting of a new stencil, it is *still* important not to allow textile paint to dry and clog in the mesh. Many general techniques are worthy of mention:

Fig. 285. Loosen Stubborn Spots With Stiff Brush

Special solvents. In the event that paint has been permitted to dry on the screen and the usual solvents and cleaning agents are not effective in removing it, the following solvents may be used (listed in order of effectiveness) : carbon tetrachloride, unleaded gasoline, xylol (sometimes called xylene). Caution should be taken when using any of these solvents that the room is well ventilated and that the skin is not unduly exposed to them. Carbon tetrachloride is *not* flammable but its vapors should not be inhaled.

Using a brush. The use of a small, stiff brush, Fig. 285, in conjunction with a solvent may aid in loosening stubborn spots of paint. Caution must be used that undue pressure is not placed on the tightly stretched silk.

Special wiping. An excellent method of simultaneously cleaning both sides of the silk is illustrated in Fig. 286. Stand the frame on its long side; using a solvent moistened rag in *each* hand, rub both sides of the silk at the same time, exerting pressure on the silk *between* the two hands. This avoids accidentally pressing one hand clear through the silk. When the stencil has been removed and even brisker rubbing can be applied to both sides of the screen, the frame is held securely with the chin, Fig. 287, while this wiping takes place.

Fig. 287. Scrub Briskly

Fig. 286. Rub Both Sides

143

Solvents

A thorough knowledge of solvents used in silk screening of textiles will assist the artist immeasurably in his work. The following table is intended as a working guide:

Substance to Dissolve	Solvent Used
Shellac	Wood alcohol or shellac thinner
Animal glue	Hot water (sometimes with a detergent)
Tusche (liquid form)	Water
Tusche (when dry)	Gasoline, benzine, kerosene
Oil base paints	Kerosene, benzine
Water base paints	Water
Lacquer film	Lacquer thinner
Stains on hands	Kerosene wash followed by strong detergent
Smudges on cloth	If cloth is white, remove as much of the smudges as possible with benzine and then bleach out the paint with a strong laundry bleach applied full strength — follow this with a vinegar wash
Hardened paint on screen	Following conventional cleaning, use carbon tetrachloride, unleaded gasoline or xylol

Care of the Hands

An artist's hands are frequently the most versatile, as well as the most valuable, set of tools he has. It is not always possible to prevent the hands from becoming smeared or stained with paints. Several excellent protective creams are available which, when rubbed well into the skin *prior to using paint,* facilitate easy cleaning of the hands after staining. Some skin is more sensitive than others to the use of harsh petroleum solvents. Such hands should be treated with cold cream after cleansing. Ordinary toilet soap can be used to fill the space under the fingernails before exposing the hands to paint. This will make it quite simple to clean the fingernails. Rubber gloves, while warm and uncomfortable, should be worn by anyone who suffers from skin allergy related to dyes and pigments.

Additional References

Biegeleisen, J. I., *Silk Screen Stencil Craft As a Hobby*. New York: Harper and Brothers Publishers, 1939.

Biegeleisen, J. I., and M. A. Cohen, *Silk Screen Techniques*. New York: Dover Publications, Inc., 1958.

Eisenberg, James, and Francis J. Kafka, *Silk Screen Printing*. Bloomington, Illinois: McKnight & McKnight Publishing Co., 1957.

Flam, David, *1001 Designs For Hand Decorating*. New York: Homecrafts, 1950.

Kosloff, Albert, *Screen Process Printing*. Cincinnati: The Signs of the Times Publishing Co., 1950.

Manual Silk Screen Printing. Chicago: Naz-Dar Co., n/d.

Stephenson, Jessie Bane, *From Old Stencils To Silk Screening*. New York: Charles Scribner's Sons, 1953.

CHAPTER 18

Novelty Decorations

For want of a better classification, the various techniques of decorating textiles with paints and dyes not easily included in the other chapters of this book will be discussed in this chapter. They are varied and many, and no attempt will be made to call the presentation complete. For the most part, they are adaptations of the freehand method, although certain of the previously explained methods play a role in these novelty decorations. Because of the freehand nature of these techniques, emphasis will be on the "spot design" rather than on repeats and over-all decorations. Chapters 3, 4, and 6 should be referred to for assistance in the development of original and free style patterns. Chapter 13 will refresh the memory of special preparations and techniques in freehand application of decoration.

Relief Painting

This technique, frequently referred to as three-dimensional coloring or liquid embroidery, is thought by some to

Fig. 288. Relief Painting on Scarf (Courtesy, CVH Laboratories Co.)

146

Fig. 289. Ties Decorated With Plastic Colors (Courtesy, CVH Laboratories Co.)

Fig. 290. Relief Painting on Black Velvet (Courtesy, CVH Laboratories Co.)

have originated in Ceylon. The decorative matter in this technique is actually raised above the surface of the fabric being decorated, Fig. 288. Therefore, the paint medium used must have a body which will adhere to the fabric, will not be absorbed into the fibers of the fabric, and which will remain attached permanently through wear and cleaning. Fig. 289 illustrates two neckties decorated with *CVH Plastic Relievo Colors*. Fig. 290 depicts a framed image decorated with the same medium on black velvet. It is obvious that this technique is readily adaptable to decorating heavy pile textiles, such as velvet, which are difficult to handle with any other paint. The technique is basically a simple one and anyone who can follow a line with a pencil can apply relief paint.

Fig. 291. Pounced Pattern (Courtesy, CVH Laboratories Co.)

Fig. 292. Paper Cone (Courtesy, CVH Laboratories Co.)

Fig. 293. Fill Cone One-Third Full (Courtesy, CVH Laboratories Co.)

The Technique

First the design is applied to the cloth. This can either be done freehand with a pencil, with a piece of pointed chalk (as explained in Chapter 7 for transferring batik designs), or by pouncing fine chalk powder or talcum powder through a pattern which has had perforations made through it* on the lines, Fig. 291. Special white pouncing powder is available for transferring patterns to dark cloth, and black pouncing powder is available for working similarly on

* pre-perforated patterns are available from dealers stocking products of the CVH Laboratories Co.

148

Fig. 294. Fold Cone Twice to Close
(Courtesy, CVH Laboratories Co.)

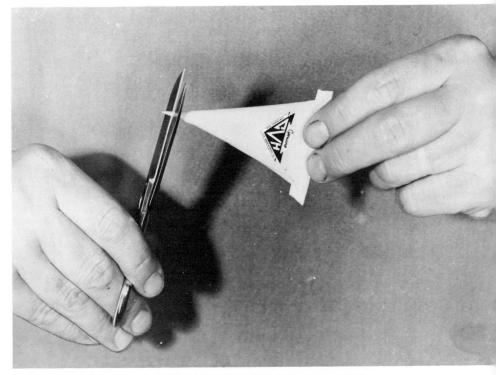

Fig. 295. Cut Small Piece From Tip (Courtesy, CVH Laboratories Co.)

light-colored cloth. A small paper cone, preferably made of glassine or other moisture-proof paper, Fig. 292, is then one-third filled with paint, Fig. 293. The cone is carefully shut by folding it over twice as shown in Fig. 294. A very small piece is cut off the end of the cone to make a small opening, Fig. 295.

Fig. 296. Follow Outline Carefully
(Courtesy, CVH Laboratories Co.)

Fig. 297. Fill Open Areas With Brush
(Courtesy, CVH Laboratories Co.)

Fig. 298. Finished Scarf (Courtesy, CVH Laboratories Co.)

Fig. 299. Fill Brush From Supply on Paper (Courtesy, CVH Laboratories Co.)

Fig. 300. Completed Tie (Courtesy, CVH Laboratories Co.)

Hold the cone in the hand and exert light pressure to force a thin stream of the paint out of the tip. Carefully go over the outlines of the design, Fig. 296. Areas within the relief outline may be filled in with color by applying the paint directly to the fabric with a flat brush, Fig. 297. The finished scarf is shown in Fig. 298. Fig. 299 illustrates the technique of fill-in painting, by applying the paint from a small amount squeezed onto a piece of paper. Fig. 300 shows a finished necktie which illustrates the outlining in three-dimensional relief paint and the shading of solid areas to give an extremely lifelike result.

Fig. 301. Decorating Luncheon Cloth (Courtesy, CVH Laboratories Co.)

These paints are available in a wide range of colors and tints, including metallic colors. Complete kits containing all of the necessary materials for practicing relief painting are available, Fig. 301.

151

Fig. 302. White Relief
Paint (Courtesy, F. Weber
Co.)

Other Products

Decora Relief, Fig. 302, is a white paint, used in the manner previously explained. It can be colored before using by mixing a quantity of it on a glass slab with a high quality, well-ground powdered tempera. After the relief paint has dried on the fabric, it can also be colored by applying *Decora-Color*, Fig. 212.

A homemade variety of relief paint can be prepared by adding a liberal quantity of dry pigment, such as *Alpha-color*, to liquid rubber (the liquid latex used for the preparation of rubber molds for plaster of Paris models). This material is used in the same manner as the aforementioned paints.

All relief paints must be completely air-dried for at least twenty-four hours before handling. They may be laundered in mild soap and warm water. Do not soak the article, and do not rub or squeeze the cloth. Rinse thoroughly in clear water and then wrap it in a dry cloth to absorb some of the moisture before drying. Iron with a moderate iron (on the reverse side) placing a clean cloth between the article and the iron.

Beads, Glitter, and Spangles

Very *fine* lustrous beads, metallic sparkle and glitter, fine sequinettes, as well as metallic bronzing powders of all shades may be applied to relief paint. These substances are applied while the paint is still tacky. Bronzing powder is applied with a soft, camel's hair brush. The other substances are applied by pouring a quantity of the substance over the painted area, Fig. 303. The ex-

cess is then poured off. Some of the metallic glitter and sequinettes, because of their heavy weight, should be carefully pressed into the tacky paint with a clean, cloth-wrapped finger.

The addition of gold and silver metallic bronze or glitter will almost impart an appearance of metallic embroidery, while the transparent glass beads transmit the basic color of the paint and add life and sparkle to the design.

Ball Point Painting

Closely akin to relief painting is ball point painting. The paint used is permanently sealed in a flexible metal tube equipped with a ball point tip similar to that used on a pen. Hold the tube as if it were a pen or a pencil, and trace over the design, Fig. 304. These paints impart a slight relief effect, depending

Fig. 304. Ball Point Painting (Courtesy, Tri-Chem, Inc.)

153

Fig. 305. Stretch Fabric Tightly (Courtesy, Tri-Chem, Inc.)

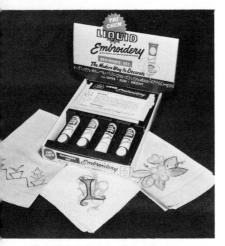

Fig. 306. Ball Point Paint Kit (Courtesy, Tri-Chem, Inc.)

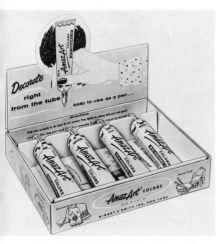

Fig. 307. Paint Kit (Courtesy, Binney & Smith, Inc.)

upon the absorption qualities of the fabric, because the paint *does* have a tendency to soak into the fibers. The paints are available ready-mixed in a palette of some twenty to thirty colors including gold and silver.

The design can be applied to the fabric with either chalk or pouncing powder as previously explained. The design can also be traced onto the cloth with carbon paper since, apparently, the wax from the carbon does not impair the adhering qualities of the paint.* The paint is very fast drying, permanently sets without heat, and can be given *gentle* laundering. After the design has been transferred, the cloth is tacked to a board very tightly or stretched in embroidery hoops as shown in Fig. 305. The paint is then applied. Since the colors dry so rapidly, additional colors can be applied next to each other almost immediately. A final air drying of twenty-four hours should be allowed before laundering.

Ball point paints are available in kits containing assorted colors, instructions for use and suggested patterns for transferring, or they may be purchased separately in any color desired, Figs. 306 and 307.

---

* When transferring a design to dark fabrics, dressmaker's carbon paper, which is available in light colors and larger than conventional sheet size, is very helpful. The white carbon paper accompanying duplicating machine stencils may also be used for this purpose.

Fig. 308. Flocked Articles (Courtesy, Vertipile, Inc.)

Flocking

Flocking is the process of applying finely cut or ground textile fibers to a surface which has been treated with an adhesive, producing a raised suede-like finish on the fabric. Its original use was limited almost entirely to the over-all coating of textiles which were then fabricated into consumer goods. Fig. 308 illustrates a collection of articles which have been given a suede-like finish. Fig. 309 shows another product which has a soft, "touchable" finish because the fabric has been flocked. Once the problems of developing adhesives to hold the flock and accurate control in the manufacturing of the flock were solved, unlimited uses for flocking were found.

The requirements for flocking are: an adhesive which will hold the fibers when they are applied under pressure, an adhesive which will be flexible

Fig. 309. Flocked Toy (Courtesy, Vertipile, Inc.)

Fig. 310. Spraying Adhesive (Courtesy, Vertipile, Inc.)

enough for normal use when dry, and a finished product which will hold its flocked finish even after laundering. Industrially, a special adhesive is sprayed onto an article, Fig. 310. The flock is then applied, either with a specially designed spray gun, or in the case of rigid

Fig. 311. Beater-Arm Application (Courtesy, Vertipile, Inc.)

articles (such as those covered with fabric) by the beater-arm method, Fig. 311. In this latter method, the beater-arm, shown in a vertical position in Fig. 311 between the operator's two hands, rotates and strikes the article intermittently so that the flock which is being sifted onto it is evenly spread.

Flocking soon became popular with the textile decorating craftsman because it had a ready application to spot designs. Sport shirts, T-Shirts, towels, kerchiefs, camp emblems (such as that shown in Fig. 312), pennants, and a variety of other articles are easily flocked.

An excellent kit, Fig. 313, and an entire line of supplies called *DonJer* is available for the home or school craftsman who desires to try this unusual method of decorating textiles. The adhesives are available in a wide range of colors. The flock is available in the same colors. Neutral, or transparent adhesive can be used with any color, but the use of a colored adhesive adds intensity to the color of the flock.

The adhesive may be applied by the stencil method (as described in Chapters 2, 3, and 4), Fig. 314, or it may be applied by the silk screen process (Chapters 14, 15, and 16), Fig. 315. It can also be applied by the freehand method, but this is not especially recommended since

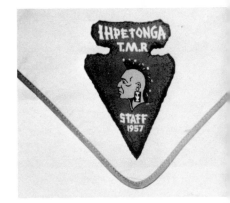

Fig. 312. Flocked Camp Emblem (Courtesy, Allied Reproduction Associates)

Fig. 313. Home Craftsman's Kit (Courtesy, DonJer Products Co.)

Fig. 314. Stenciling Adhesive

Fig. 315. Screening Adhesive

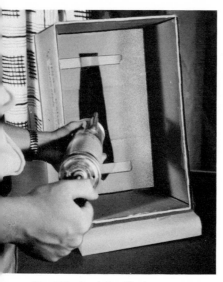

Fig. 316. Applying Flock

the adhesive must be flocked as soon as possible after application. The freehand method is slower, and some of the adhesive may dry out and not hold the flock.

The kit in Fig. 313 also contains a special high-pressure gun operated by hand. All that is necessary to apply the flock is to fill the chamber in the gun with the flock and fasten the article (with adhesive applied) to the inside of a cardboard carton which will serve as a spraying shield, and "shoot" the flock onto it, Fig. 316. After the application, the excess flock is shaken off into the box. It is all gathered together and is replaced in the container. The article must be completely air-dried overnight. Mild laundering is recommended.

Universal Pigments

These are usually dry color pigments which can be added to a wide variety of vehicles for use in the decoration of an equally wide variety of materials. This type of pigment is classified in this chapter because it is valuable to the artist who does not care to invest in many sets of different paints and pigments, each serving *one* specific method of application. *Alpha-Color Craftmix* is one such vehicle. It is a white, creamy substance which mixes easily with dry pigments to make a waterproof paint that can be applied in many different ways. It will never harden, settle, spoil, or separate, no mattter how long it is exposed to the air. This is of great value, especially in silk screening because the screen will not clog while working. After it has been applied, it is made launder proof by heat-setting at approximately

158

350 degrees Fahrenheit, as explained in other chapters. *Craftmix* is non-toxic, odorless, and is easily wiped off the hands with a cloth. Remaining quantities of the mixture can be stored indefinitely, even in an open container.

Transferring Pictures to Cloth

Almost any *printed pictures*, but especially those printed on a highly absorbent paper such as newsprint can be transferred to cloth. This may be desirable occasionally as a novelty gift, particularly if someone's picture appears in a newspaper or magazine.

Dissolve approximately one-quarter ounce of pure soap flakes in two ounces of boiling water. Allow the solution to cool, and slowly stir in two ounces of pure spirits of turpentine. Cut the picture from the newspaper or magazine and soak it carefully in this solution by brushing both sides of the paper with a wide, soft brush. Carefully blot off excess moisture between two paper towels. Place the wet picture face down on the clean, flat cloth to be imprinted. Place a paper towel on top of the inverted picture and rub over the entire back with the bowl end of a soup spoon. Carefully remove the paper picture, it will have transferred itself to the cloth. Allow the cloth to thoroughly air dry until no further odor of turpentine is noticeable (about 24 hours). Cloth so printed may be washed in mild soap and warm water and ironed on the reverse side.

Photographic emulsions are difficult to transfer because they will not offset (soften and "print off") the way printing inks do. This process usually involves the making of a silver nitrate photographic emulsion, sensitizing the cloth with it, drying it in darkness, and then printing directly onto it with a negative, and proceeding to process it as any other photograph. The entire technique is much too involved to make the result worth the effort.

Additional References

Cox, Doris, and Barbara Warren Weisman, *Creative Hands*. New York: John Wiley & Sons, Inc., 1945.

Design Technics. Columbus, Ohio: Design Publishing Co., n/d.

Flock Finishing For Decorative & Functional Purposes. Troy, New York: Behr-Manning, 1949.

Paint It Yourself. West End, New Jersey: CVH Laboratories Co., 1950.

Parisi, Tony, *Craftsman's Instruction Handbook*. New York: Educational Materials, Inc., 1945.

CHAPTER 19

Color and Color Mixing

A great deal of confusion exists concerning color and color mixing, and there are times when the artist and the home craftsman feel that any color can be given almost *any* identification.

General Information

The important thing to keep in mind in all explorations into the study of color is that there are *three primary (or basic) colors*. Where these are obtained, how they are made, or what makes them appear the way they do are studies for advanced research workers. These *primary colors* are red, yellow, and blue. By mixing *equal parts of any two* of these colors, the *secondary colors* are produced. Thus, by mixing equal parts of red and yellow, *orange* is produced. Equal parts of yellow and blue produce *green*. Equal parts of red and blue produce *violet*. Therefore, orange, green, and violet are the *secondary* colors.

For the beginner it is best to always call a *red* a *red*, an *orange* an *orange*, etc., regardless of whether it is lighter

161

or darker than others which can be found. This holds true for all the *primary* and *secondary colors:* red, orange, yellow, green, blue, violet.

Mixing Secondary Colors

By using the following table, the two colors required to produce the secondary color can be found. Locate the secondary color desired. Run the finger straight across the line to the left end column and the *one* primary color will be located. Run the finger straight up the column from the secondary color and at the top will be found the *second* color required for the mixture. By mixing equal parts the secondary color will be produced.

TO MIX SECONDARY COLORS

	RED	YELLOW	BLUE
RED		Orange	Violet
YELLOW	Orange		Green
BLUE	Violet	Green	

The above table is also useful in determining what the resulting color may be when printing on textiles, in the event that one primary color is printed over another primary color. This is true of almost all dyes, inks, and transparent textile colors (particularly yellow), which have been "thinned down" for silk screen printing.

Tints and Shades

A *tint of a color* is produced by adding *pure white* to any one of the six colors mentioned in the above table. An elementary characteristic of light governs the fact that adding white to a color *increases its light value*. In other words, *more light is reflected* back to the eyes resulting in an appearance of brightness. Thus, when white is added to red, pink is produced.

A *shade of color* is produced by adding *absolute black* to any of the colors above. The *light value decreases* with the addition of black. *Less light is reflected* back to the eyes, thus creating an impression of the color being darker. When *black* is added to red, a dull maroon or burgundy color is produced.

The following table will assist in determining how tints and shades are produced. The primary and secondary colors are listed across the top of the table. White and black are listed in the left-hand column. The shades and tints (by the names most usually recognized) appear where the horizontal and vertical columns intersect, as in the previous table.

TO MIX SHADES AND TINTS

	RED	ORANGE	YELLOW	GREEN	BLUE	VIOLET
WHITE	Pink	Flesh	Pale Yellow	Leaf Green	Pale Blue	Orchid
BLACK	Maroon	Salmon	Olive Drab	Deep Green	Navy Blue	Lavender

The intermediate color of *gray is produced* by adding *black to white* until the desired *gray* is produced.

Some of the names for colors appearing in the table just above may be questioned by artists other than the author. A serious attempt has been made, however, to omit thoroughly confusing colors found in shops dealing in wearing apparel. It must also be kept in mind that, when mixing tints or shades, a complete *range of a tint* is created by adding more and more of the color to the white. In like manner an entire *range of shades* is created by adding increasingly large quantities of black to a color. The confusion which exists in color classification usually exists within the framework of shades and tints.

Tertiary Colors

The *tertiary colors* (or third order colors) are produced by mixing *equal parts of any two secondary colors*. It is readily seen that this is the same as mixing *unequal parts* of any two *primary colors*. Thus, if green and orange are mixed in equal parts the resulting color will be *brown*. Since green contains equal parts of blue and yellow, and orange contains equal parts of yellow and red, then brown actually contains *unequal parts* of red, yellow, and blue. The addition of white to a tertiary color will produce tints of that color and the addition of black will produce shades. Hence, it is easily seen that almost unlimited ranges of colors are possible with a supply of red, yellow, blue, white, and black.

Dyeing Textiles

When using dyes, such as in batik, home dyeing, or in other techniques where liquid dyes, stains, and inks are used, the colors produced by dyeing one color over another are *not always as accurate* a combination as the previous two tables would indicate. For one thing, white as a pigment is not available in transparent dye form. To create tints

164

with liquid dyes, more water is added to the color or the fabric is dyed for a shorter period of time (refer to Chapter 7, "The Art of Batik"). Certain colors also have a much heavier pigmentation and are therefore less transparent than others. Black is usually so intense that it will cover almost any other color and generally produce a black appearance.

The table in Fig. 317 is a reasonably accurate reference chart (used in the same manner as the two previous tables) for determining the color produced when a textile article of one color is *dyed* with another color. This chart is only applicable to transparent dyes — not to opaque paints. Dyes can also be combined, either in the raw state or after mixing with water, to produce secondary and tertiary colors. However,

	Over RED Produces	Over BLUE Produces	Over YELLOW Produces	Over BROWN Produces	Over ORANGE Produces	Over GREEN Produces	Over PURPLE Produces
RED	DARKER RED	PURPLE	SCARLET	REDDISH BROWN	LIGHT RED	DULL BROWN	REDDISH PURPLE
BLUE	PURPLE	DEEP BLUE	GREEN	VERY DARK BROWN	DULL DARK GRAY	BOTTLE GREEN	BLUISH PURPLE
YELLOW	SCARLET	GREEN	DEEP YELLOW	GOLDEN BROWN	YELLOW ORANGE	LIGHT GREEN	GREENISH BROWN
BROWN	BROWNISH RED	ALMOST BLACK	YELLOWISH BROWN	DARKER BROWN	YELLOWISH DARK BROWN	DULL GREENISH BROWN	CHOCOLATE
ORANGE	LIGHT RED	DULL DARK GRAY	LIGHT ORANGE	TOBACCO BROWN	DEEP ORANGE	YELLOWISH GREEN	RED DISH BROWN
GREEN	ALMOST BLACK	GREENISH BLUE	LIGHT GREEN	OLIVE GREEN	MYRTLE GREEN	DARKER GREEN	DULL DARK GREEN
PURPLE	REDDISH PURPLE	PLUM	ALMOST BLACK	VERY DARK REDDISH BROWN	LIGHT DULL PURPLE	DULL DARK PURPLE	DARKER PURPLE

Fig. 317. Color Chart for Dyeing (Courtesy, The Monroe Chemical Co., makers of "Putnam Dyes.")

because of the varying intensity of different colors, it is best for the artist to refer to a reference manual published by the manufacturer of the dye.

Because certain shades, tints, and tertiary colors have become reasonably fixed in the minds of consumers, the following *selected list* is offered as a guide. The names of some popular colors are highly debatable from a technical point of view, but by *common usage* have become established. Next to each color are the component colors required to produce it. Beyond this point the artist should experiment for himself.

Dresden Blue	White, blue, a touch of violet
Gun Metal	Gray with a touch of blue and a touch of red
Mustard	White, yellow, a touch of red and black
Beige	White with a touch of tan
Chartreuse	Yellow with a touch of blue
Turquoise	White, blue, and a touch of yellow
Rose	White, red, and a touch of blue
Sand	Tint *beige* with white
Gold (non-metallic)	Tint *mustard* with white

Additional References

Bustanoby, J. H., *Principles of Color and Color Mixing*. New York: McGraw-Hill Book Co., 1947.

Charm of Color, The. Quincy, Illinois: Monroe Chemical Co., 1948.

Information File On Home Dyeing. New York: Tintex Home Economics Bureau, 1957.

CHAPTER 20

Home Dyeing

The origins of dyeing fabric, or the process of transferring color to cloth, whether in a particular design technique or not, are lost in antiquity. Garments exquisitely colored with indigo have been found in Thebes that date from approximately 3,500 B. C. Older evidences (as early as 25,000 B. C.) indicate that man was familiar with coloring pigments when painting his caves. It is a fair assumption that these pigments were used on cloth as soon as it was invented. The earliest dyes were undoubtedly of vegetable origin, although minerals, particularly iron oxide, were used.

Mordanting, or the process of *fixing the coloring pigments* permanently to the fibers of the cloth, was known very early in man's technical development. The use of tannic acid (derived from oak tree bark and leaves) and cowdung (animal derivative) as mordants is still practiced in the ancient manner in India. Alum, derived from potash, is also used as a mordant. With these mordants, the brilliant colors of the pomegranate fruit (yellow) and the madder plant root (red), were made permanent in cotton fibers.

Vegetable Dyes

Vegetable dyes were not always colorfast. This fact together with irregular control of mordanting has resulted in a loss of many samples of this ancient art. The following are some vegetable dyes which were used, and still are used in parts of the world, for dyeing fabric:

Indigo. A plant grown mainly in tropical climates. A brilliant, colorfast, blue dye is derived from the leaves.

Saffron. A plant grown extensively by the ancient Greeks and Romans. The pistils of the flower are used to produce a yellow dye.

Brazilwood. One of the redwood trees. A brilliant red dye is extracted from the wood.

Logwood. A large tropical tree whose wood produces a range of dyes in the purple, violet, and black classifications.

Orseille. This is a lichen which grows in Mediterranean countries. The heads of the stems produce a purple color.

With the white of cotton and linen fibers, a fair range of coloring substances were known to ancient peoples.

Animal Dyes

Animal dyes were known to ancient man; but, due to their rarity, they were always expensive and used only by the rich. Their colors apparently were more intense and showed a greater colorfastness. Some of these are:

Shellfish. An expensive purple dye was extracted from the bodies of various shellfish in Crete and Tyre.

Kermes. An oriental louse, living on leaves of low shrubs. Its dry powdered body yielded a bright scarlet dye.

Cochineal. An insect found in Mexico, living very often on cactus plants. The juices in its body are still used for producing a bright red dye.

Mineral Dyes

Mineral dyes were very rare in antiquity. Some people in various parts of the world did discover that cloth could be tinted by dipping it in springs and streams rich in iron compounds. The ancient Egyptians also used oxidized copper for a green dye, and azurite for a blue dye. Certain native earths colored with iron oxide yielded ochres of yellow and tan.

It is interesting to note that in Colonial America iron scraps were immersed in a barrel of water and vinegar (the mordant). The resulting liquid was used as a dye bath for the somewhat drab, monotonous brown and tan found in their early fabrics.

Modern Dyes

Modern dyeing methods began in 1856 when aniline, derived from coal tar, was discovered to be capable of producing a wide range of colors when chemically treated. Little by little, man has been released from his dependency on vegetable and animal dyes. Modern dyes are easy to mix and use, usually contain their own mordant (or require the addition of a simple one like table salt or vinegar), are colorfast to light and laundering, will dye *all* kinds of fibers (including the synthetic ones), and are inexpensive. Most modern dyes are fast in their functioning and can be applied without boiling. This last feature is important since boiling can cause serious damage to wool fibers and some synthetics. So colorfast are modern household dyes that even *tinting*, the process of immersing the fabric in a lukewarm, diluted dye bath, creates a light shade or tint in permanent color.

Preparation for Dyeing

All articles should be thoroughly clean and free from stains. If the fabric has already been formed into an article of wearing apparel, hems should be open and buttons and buckles removed. If the article is faded, spotted, or unevenly dyed from a previous dyeing, the color should be completely removed with a special bleach manufactured by the maker of the dye. Unless the fabric is deliberately being *overdyed* to produce a different color (see Chapter 19), it is recommended that it be bleached first.

The vessel used for dyeing should be agate, enamel, or stainless steel. Iron, galvanized iron, aluminum, and copper vessels should not be used because these metals impart impurities which have a harmful effect on the dye. The dyeing vessel should be large enough to hold the amount of fabric without crowding. The amount of water used is not important since the fabric will "take up" the amount of dye which has been added, regardless of the quantity of water into which it has been dissolved. A smooth stick, a large wooden spoon, or a large stainless steel spoon, will be needed for stirring and handling the article in the dye bath. A quart glass jar or pitcher for dissolving the dye will be needed. This can also be enamel ware or stainless steel, although glass enables easy observation of the dissolving process.

Procedure

1. If the fabric to be dyed has not just been washed and rinsed, then rinse it thoroughly in clear water and place it aside wet.

2. Stir the powdered dye in the quart container of hot tap water until it is completely dissolved. Some colors dissolve more slowly than others. The quantity of dye needed for a given quantity of fabric (by weight in ounces and pounds) is furnished by the manufacturer. The use of less dye than recommended will produce lighter shades and tints. The use of more dye will produce darker ranges. However, it is strongly recommended that darker shades be obtained by using the darker ranges of colors ready-mixed and available.

3. Fill the dyeing vessel with cold water in sufficient quantity to cover the fabric completely. A good method of determining this is to place the fabric in the dyeing vessel, fill it to the proper depth, remove the fabric, wring excess water back into the vessel, and place the wet fabric aside.

4. Place the dyeing vessel on the stove to begin heating it. Immediately

Fig. 318. Adding Dissolved Dye to Water (Courtesy, Park & Tilford, makers of "Tintex")

Fig. 319. Immerse Wet Fabric in Dye Solution (Courtesy, Park & Tilford, makers of "Tintex")

Fig. 320. Rinse Until Water is Clear

add the dissolved dye to the water in the dyeing vessel, stirring it as it is added, Fig. 318.

5. Place the wet fabric, unfolded, into the dye bath, so that it is completely immersed in the solution, Fig. 319.

6. Heat the dye bath until it is *just below* the boiling point (approximately 200° Fahrenheit if a technical thermometer is used). Constantly stir the fabric around in the dye bath to permit even dyeing. Heat for the time specified by the dye manufacturer (usually 20 to 30 minutes). Turn off the heat and allow the fabric to remain in the dye bath until it is lukewarm, continuing to stir it regularly.

7. Rinse the fabric in cold running water until the water remains clear, Fig. 320. The fabric may be squeezed and wrung by hand during this rinsing process, Fig. 321, but the use of rubber gloves is recommended.

Additional Hints

1. Fabric which has absorbed the full intensity of the color, and thus the full amount of the dye, will be completely dyed when the dye bath water turns almost clear again. The heating time required for this to take place will vary with the color being used and the kind of fiber being dyed.

2. Shorter periods in the dye bath will produce lighter shades and tints. Some colors also appear lighter or darker on different fibers. It is suggested, where a great deal of

172

dyeing is done over a period of time, or when the same color depth is desired at a later date, that a sample swatch of material be added to the dye bath. The sample should be cut from the same fabric (in case of a finished article a piece may be cut from the hem). The quantity of dye used and the length of time in the dye bath should be noted on a label which is pasted to the sample swatch. It will also be noticed that dyed fabrics look darker when wet than they do after drying.

3. If vinegar or table salt are specified as mordants to be added to the dye, these substances should be added at that point specified by the manufacturer (usually just before the fabric is immersed into the dye bath).

4. Stains in the sink and in dyeing vessels can be removed with a good household bleach or with a solution of the color removing bleach made by the same company manufacturing the dye.

Fig. 321. Rubber Gloves Are Recommended

Dyeing In a Regular Washing Machine

1. Preheat the machine by allowing the hottest water possible to remain standing in it for 15 minutes.

2. Fill the machine with very hot water to the level required to completely cover the fabric. Place the pre-washed and rinsed fabric into the machine unfolded.

3. Carefully pour the dissolved dye into the machine, Fig. 322, making sure that none of it is poured directly onto the fabric.

Fig. 322. Add Dissolved Dye — Do Not Pour Directly on Fabric (Courtesy, Park & Tilford, makers of "Tintex")

Fig. 323. Washing Cycle Should Operate Twice (Courtesy, Westinghouse Electric Corp.)

4. Turn on the machine and allow it to run for 20 to 30 minutes. Rinse in cold water, as with hand dyeing, until *bleeding* of color stops.
5. Do not wring the fabric or run it through the wringer.

Dyeing In an Automatic Washer

1. While the machine is filling with water, dissolve the dye as previously explained in a quart container.
2. Immerse the fabric in the water until completely covered. Then add the dye to the water so that none is poured directly onto the fabric.
3. Let the machine operate during the regular *washing* cycle, Fig. 323. Repeat the washing cycle once or twice to accomplish the necessary dyeing time.
4. Set the machine on the *last* rinse and rinse the fabric until water is clear.
5. If a spin dryer is available the fabric may be spun dry. Otherwise remove it wet, squeeze excess moisture out and hang it to dry. Do not wring it or run it through a wringer.

Additional References

Charm of Color, The. Quincy, Illinois: Monroe Chemical Co., 1948.
Information File On Home Dyeing. New York: Tintex Home Economics Bureau, 1957.

CHAPTER 21

Caring for Decorated Fabrics

The care normally given to any fine, delicate fabric is all the care necessary for decorated fabrics. Special care to be given fabrics which have been decorated in unusual ways, such as batik and relief painting, has been discussed in previous chapters. Home-dyed fabrics which have been colored in a heated dye can usually be given much harsher treatment. Normally the fabrics which have been hand decorated are those which will not be abused in use and, therefore, do not need strong detergents, extremely hot water, or other harsh treatment for proper cleaning. The specific instructions for cleaning, washing, laundering, ironing, given by the manufacturer of the paint or dye, as well as the maker of the fabric itself, should always be followed. The following instructions are offered for their *general value* as a guide.

Washing

Hand decorated fabrics should *never* be boiled or subjected to ammonia, caustic soda, or other harsh bleaches while washing. They should not be soaked any longer than absolutely necessary to soften dirt and soiled spots. Wherever possible, localized stains and spots should be removed, or at least softened, with a dry cleaning agent or thick detergent suds prior to soaking. Always use a mild soap and water which is no hotter than the naked hand can tolerate. A mild detergent may also be used, but the liquid variety is preferred. The fabric should not be wrung and stretched or otherwise subjected to rough treatment. Except for certain of the silk screened articles and those stencilled with a *commercial* paint, all hand decorated fabrics should be washed by hand, and not by machine. Batik articles must be washed in water which is merely lukewarm. A good guide as to whether a fabric may be machine washed is to examine it to determine if the paint penetrated clear through to the reverse of the cloth. If so, it is usually safe to wash by machine. No hand decorated fabric should be twist-wrung by hand, but rather it should be squeezed. *All* but relief paint decorated fabrics may be machine wrung, Fig. 324, with the cloth in a folded rather than twisted position.

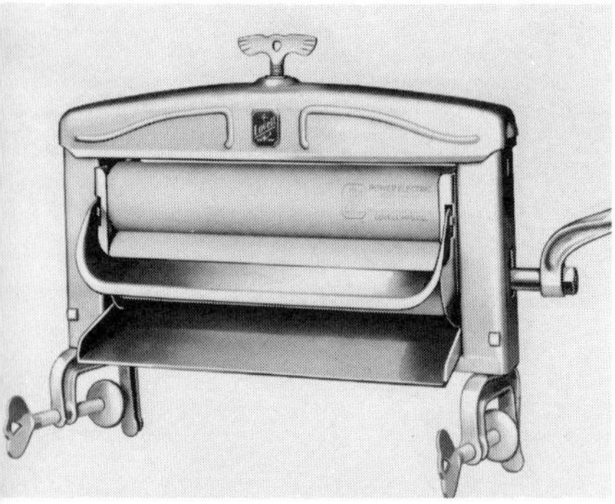

Dry-Cleaning

A good quality dry-cleaning, commonly referred to as "French" dry-cleaning, is recommended for *all* of the fabrics decorated with *commercially* obtained paints. Dry-cleaning is preferred to washing for batiks. Home-dyed articles may be dry-cleaned without risk. Block printed, hand stenciled, and hand painted fabrics, which have been deco-

Fig. 324. If Wringer Is Used, Fold Fabric Carefully (Courtesy, Lovell Manufacturing Co.)

176

rated with homemade pigments, mordants, etc., (all of which are mixtures of printer's inks or artist's colors) are preferably washed rather than being dry-cleaned. It is recommended that certain articles, such as batiks and those decorated with relief paints, be ironed or pressed at home even if commercially dry-cleaned.

Ironing and Pressing

Two rules are basic to all ironing of hand decorated fabrics:

1. A pressing cloth should always be used, Fig. 325. It is wet, wrung dry, and placed flat against the fabric between the iron and the fabric being ironed. In the case of dry ironing, a damp cloth may be used. When a steam iron is used, the cloth may be dry. In either case, steaming makes it possible to remove wrinkles with lower temperatures and less pressure.

2. The temperature of the iron must be regulated for the type of fabric being ironed. This is extremely important in hand decorated work since scorching cannot be bleached out without damaging the decorations and may completely ruin a fabric which took hours to decorate. Most electric irons are adjustable for various temperatures, Fig. 326. The adjustment control may be calibrated for temperature degrees, type of fabric, or just in "high," "medium," and "low" readings. The following table combines all three sets of calibrations.

Fig. 325. Pressing Cloth Should Be Used (Courtesy, Westinghouse Electric Corp.)

Fig. 326. Steam Iron (Courtesy, General Electric Corp.)

177

Type of fabric	Degree reading	Temperature reading
Rayon	240 degrees F.	Low
Nylon	240 degrees F.	Low
Dacron	240 degrees F.	Low
Silk	300 degrees F.	Medium
Wool	360 degrees F.	Medium
Cotton	420 degrees F.	High
Linen	480 degrees F.**	High(est)

**Linen is best ironed when still quite damp.

CHAPTER 22

Sources of Supply

Since sources of supply change so frequently in local areas, and also vary from one geographical region to another, it is suggested that the artist, teacher, student, or home craftsman use his local classified telephone directory as a guide. The following headings which may be found in this directory will be helpful in locating a dealer.

Artists' Materials
Arts & Crafts Supplies
Brushes
Chemicals — Manufacturers & Distributors
Cleaning Compounds
Cotton Goods — Wholesale
Dress Goods
Dry Goods Stores
Dry Goods — Wholesale
Dyes & Dyestuffs
Linens — Decorative & Household
Linens — Piece Goods
Linoleum Dealers
Paint Manufacturers & Distributors
Paint & Painter's Supplies — Dealers
Paint & Varnish Removers — Dealers
Paint & Varnish Removers — Manufacturers
Printing Inks
Printing Supplies
Rayon Fabrics
Signs — Equipment & Supplies
Silk Screen Processing
Silk Screen Processing Equip. & Supplies
Solvents
Stencils & Stencil Supplies
Stationers
Textile Mill Supplies
Textile Printing
Textile Reproductions
Textile Finishing
Textile Fibers

Most manufacturers do not like to sell directly to the consumer because this practice violates contracts which they have made with the distributors of their products. Manufacturers will, however, usually furnish the name and address of an authorized distributor in any given locality.

CHAPTER 23

A Gallery of Samples

The following pages will give the home or school artist and craftsman a broad overview of the kinds of articles which can be decorated. These illustrations depict outstanding samples of contemporary artists' and craftsmen's work, using most of the methods and techniques discussed in the book. Some of the illustrations show merely the spot or repeat design itself, as applied to textile fabric, allowing the craftsman free choice of what to fabricate from the decorated material. Other illustrations show the finished products. Ready-made designs for the beginner can be obtained in any one of the several books mentioned at the end of the various sections of this book. It is hoped that the beginner will practice *creativity* in design right from the start using methods described in Chapters 3 through 6. Even a quick glance at some of the samples which follow will stimulate the creative craftsman.

Fig. 327. (Courtesy, American Crayon Co.)

A Variety of Projects (Various Techniques)

Fig. 327. A variety of decorated textile projects made by convalescents at Billings General Hospital, Ft. Harrison, Indiana. Most of the articles are stenciled, a few are hand painted.

Fig. 328. A series of projects which, when hand decorated, add sparkle and interest to otherwise purely utilitarian objects. From left to right: a dish towel, stenciled in over-all repeat; a child's dress with appliques of block printed

Fig. 328. (Courtesy, American Crayon Co.)

Fig. 329. (Courtesy, American Crayon Co.)

rectangles; an apron with an over-all repeat in stencil; another apron with a broad border repeat.

Fig. 329. On the left are two over-all repeat patterns, applicable to slip-cover or drapery fabrics, done in silk screen — either lacquer film or tusche glue. In the upper right is a matching set of child's bib and finger towel in stencil method. Lower right shows a pull-string handbag and inner change purse made of matching fabrics silk screened in an over-all repeat in two colors.

182

Fig. 330. (Courtesy, American Crayon Co.)

Fig. 331. (Courtesy, American Crayon Co.)

Stenciling (Chapters 2, 3, 4, 5, 6)

Fig. 330. A hand stenciled place mat executed in five colors. Note the shading technique and the abstract figuration in the heads and faces.

Fig. 331. Hand stenciled spot design. Applicable to napkins and corners of luncheon sets as well as to border repeats. Traditionally accomplished in one color, with shading technique lending variance in color depth.

Fig. 332. Child's pinafores decorated with the stencil technique to accent color. The one on the left illustrates a multicolored spot design with a repeat border, while the one at the right depicts an over-all repeat on the front and a pocket over-all repeat sewed on, *after stenciling.*

Fig. 332. (Courtesy, American Crayon Co.)

183

Fig. 333. (Courtesy, American Crayon Co.)

Fig. 333. Two excellent examples of over-all repeats utilizing the shading technique as well as multicolor to give variety. Note in the left-hand illustration the use of the *inverted repeat,* while in the right-hand sample the repeat is a full-drop, using *two separate patterns, each* of which accomplished a full repeat.

Fig. 334. A holiday gift package in which the wide ribbon has been hand stenciled. In this instance, the ribbon is silver with a stenciling of red and blue. Basically, this is an over-all repeat pattern which can be used on *wider fabric.*

Fig. 334. (Courtesy, American Crayon Co.)

Fig. 335

Batik (Chapters 7, 8)

Fig. 335. A professionally hand dyed batik in four colors. Note that "crackling" (in which the wax is permitted to solidify and is then cracked prior to bathing in the dye) and "spattering" (in which the hot wax is spattered on the fabric prior to immersion in the dye) have both been utilized, in addition to conventional brush application of the wax. Batik is a relatively rare art, as practiced today. It is worth the artist's time to investigate "outdoor" art shows and college and university art exhibits if he is interested in "first-hand" samples of this fast-disappearing art.

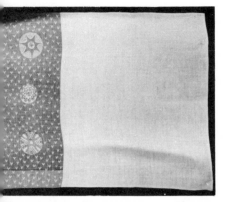

Block Prints (Chapters 10, 11, 12)

Fig. 336. A block printed luncheon mat, accomplished in one color. An over-all repeat of background motif has been combined with a spot design immersed in this background motif. Linen, the traditional fiber of luncheon service, was used.

Fig. 337. An interesting block print, done with a linoleum block, which utilizes an over-all repeat motif used in a *specific area.* Frequently a block which has been cut for use on an over-all repeat for drapery or slip-cover material, can be used within a restricted area (such as the one illustrated) to produce a bold and sophisticated design.

Fig. 338. In this illustration, a hostess apron has been decorated with block printing in combination with an application of ric-rac. The pockets of the apron are applied after imprinting with the same block. A solid, single color has been used to create this dramatic design.

Fig. 337. (Courtesy, **The American Home Magazine**)

Fig. 338. (Courtesy, American Crayon Co.)

Fig. 339. A border repeat consisting of *two separate blocks* was used to create this stylized version of an old Pennsylvania-German motif. The border makes up *one block,* printed around a luncheon cloth or dinner cloth. The "proud rooster" motif with the inner border line is imprinted with a second block. Both blocks may imprint from the same color plate or each may be printed in a different color.

Fig. 339. Courtesy, **The American Home Magazine**)

Hand Painting and Relief Painting (Chapters 13, 18)

Figs. 340 and 341. (Courtesy, CVH Laboratories Co.)

Fig. 340. Neckties painted in relief paints with a combination of "fill-in" in planographic coloring. Note the individuality of each tie. Silk or nylon were the fabrics used.

Fig. 341. Additional neckties illustrating a wide variance in brush techniques and the use of six or more colors. A definite three dimensional effect is created through the deft use of color, in the total range of tints and shades.

Fig. 342. (Courtesy, CVH Laboratories Co.)

Fig. 342. An elaborately decorated "doily", definitely in the *overdecorated school* of applied design, yet nontheless demonstrating the third dimensional effect possible with freehand brush techniques and relief paint applications.

Fig. 343. (Courtesy, American Crayon Co.)

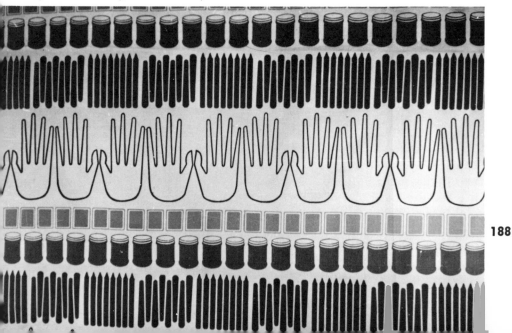

188

Silk Screen Printing (Chapters 14, 15, 16, 17)

Fig. 343. An abstract, stylized pattern, utilizing the hands and materials of the craftsman, as symbolized at the studios of the American Crayon Company. This over-all repeat is accomplished in lacquer film silk screen and produces drapery fabric and even upholstery fabric, for informal settings.

Fig. 344. A souvenir kerchief silk screened in three colors. Note the perfect registry between any two colors. The pigments used in producing this article (fast drying lacquers) assure colorfastness through ordinary laundering methods.

Fig. 345. An over-all repeat, silk screen printed, place mat, made with tusche-glue method. Note the free flowing line technique. This article, printed in opaque white on a deep green linen, does not give as complete colorfastness as some deeper-penetrating pigments.

Fig. 346. An over-all repeat, lacquer film silk screen print in two colors. Black and red on a *natural linen* were combined to create this smart and informal drapery fabric for a den or informal "dinette."

Fig. 344

Fig. 345. (Courtesy, American Crayon Co.)

Fig. 346. (Courtesy, American Crayon Co.)

189

Fig. 348. (Courtesy, American Crayon Co.)

Fig. 347. (Courtesy, American Crayon Co.)

Fig. 349. (Courtesy, American Crayon Co.)

Fig. 347. Bold, vigorous, repeat patterns printed in black, gray, and brown create this startling silk screen repeat. Lacquer film technique with a carefully planned register give an almost primitive grandeur to this pattern.

Fig. 348. Modern, yet acceptably eclectic, might be the best description for this motif. The butterflies are printed in black, over a freehand, lacquer-film-screened background. The background is in two colors over a white fabric which creates a four-color fabric of great beauty.

Fig. 349. A dress fabric, printed prior to fabrication into a skirt, has modern sophistication in two colors on white, which silk screen is capable of producing. Tan and deep russet are the colors used on this white, crush-proof cotton weave.

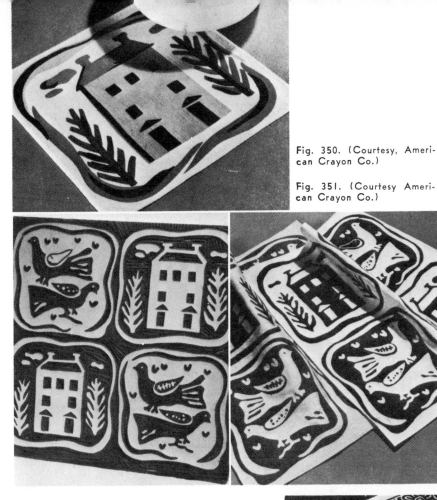

Fig. 350. A bold example of *simple* design, almost reminiscent of an early American print, in which the bare, primitive lines, create the interest. Printed in two colors, by lacquer film silk screen, on linen place mats.

Fig. 351. A similar "primitive" technique, almost a block print, executed in *one bright color* with lacquer film silk screen in an over-all repeat on Irish linen dish towels.

Fig. 352. An intricate, charming and fascinating repeat pattern, created with tusche-glue silk screen. Printed onto

Fig. 352. (Courtesy, American Crayon Co.)

Fig. 353. (Courtesy, American Crayon Co.)

Fig. 354. (Courtesy, American Crayon Co.)   Fig. 355. (Courtesy, American Crayon Co.

tightly-woven cotton napkins and luncheon cloth, in one color, this design lends simplicity and impressiveness at the same time.

Fig. 353. A heavy "monks' cloth" or "butchers' linen" has been screened in black paint from a simply cut lacquer film silk screen stencil, to create this dramatic and pleasing pillow cover.

Fig. 354. A fine-lined technique, best accomplished in lacquer film, produces a luncheon cloth of rare beauty. A "patch" of not more than four by six inches, used as a continuous repeat, can produce this type of over-all pattern.

Fig. 355. This striking shirt-front is silk screened in one color. Cut-out patches of

192

paper were applied to the silk, as described in the latter portion of Chapter 14. The cuffs were cut from random pieces of fabric printed from the same screen.

Fig. 356. Strictly a novelty item, neckties are silk screened by the hundreds, in two colors over a colored fabric to create a three-color design. This type of utilitarian article is possible without much effort when the silk screen, lacquer film technique is mastered.

Fig. 357. A batik design from the island of Java. In former days Sultans and princes had their own designs which no other person could wear. An Indonesian distinguishes a man by the design in his sarong.

Fig. 356. (Courtesy, American Crayon Co.)

Fig. 357. (Courtesy, Republic of Indonesia Information Office, New York City)

Index

Abstract design, developing, 17
Adhering lacquer film stencil, 120
Adhesive for flocking, 155
 applying, 157
Aniline dyes, 169
Animal dyes, 168
Azurite, 169
Ballpoint painting, 153

Batik, 1, 4, 5, 41-57
 handkerchief, 53-57
Batik fabrics, washing, 176
Beads, 152
Beater arm method of flocking, 157
Bench hook, for cutting blocks, 77
Bleaching, before dyeing, 170
Block printing, 1, 67-93
 basic method, 67, 68
 design renderings, 75
 novelty techniques, 89-93
Block prints, early, 89
Border repeat
 laying out, 22
 stenciling, 20-24
Bottle caps, printing from, 92
Bottle corks, printing from, 92
Boxwood, 89
Brayer, 79
Brazilwood, 168
Broad stripe, in tie dyeing, 60, 64
Bronzing powder, 152
Brush
 camel's hair, 152
 in silk screen, 143
 for stenciling, 12
Burlap, as printing surface, 92

Carving tools, 71
Chalk, use in developing batik
 design, 46
Cleanliness, in silk screen, 142
Cloth
 preparing for batik, 54

preparing for decorating, 24
preparing for freehand work, 96
preparing long length for
 printing, 36
preparing for stenciling, 14
Cochineal, 169
Color chart for dyeing, 165
Colors
 in batik, 53
 choosing, 28, 29
 and color mixing, 161-166
 in freehand work, 99
 mixing popular, 166
 registering in silk screen, 128-138
 sequence of application, 30
 sequence in batik, 47
 for silk screen, 139
 in tie dyeing, 62-64
Copper oxide, 169
Cords, for tie dyeing, 60
Cork prints, 92
Crackle pattern, in batik, 50

Da-Glo pigments, 141
Decorated fabrics, caring for,
 175-178
Designing
 abstract, 17
 for batik, 54
 for block printing, 74
 cut paper techniques, 21
 freeform, 17
 with geometric forms, 33
 in register, 131
 for silk screening, 114
 for tie dyeing, 59
Designs
 in batik, 5
 in block print, 3
 characteristics of batik, 42, 52
 developing for stenciling, 16
 limitations of stencil, 9
 reversing for block printing, 76

Designs *(con't)*
  in tie dye, 5
  transferring batik to fabric, 48
Detergents, and decorated fabrics, 176
Dry-cleaning, decorated fabrics, 176
Drying, silk screen prints, 123
Dye bath, preparing, 62
Dyeing, 1, 62, 63
  basic procedure, 171
  in batik, 51
  color chart for, 165
  history, 167
  home, 167-174
  preparations for, 170
  preserving samples of, 52
  textiles, 164
Dyes
  aniline, 169
  animal, 168
  for batik, 45
  mineral, 169
  vegetable, 168

Electroplate, 70
Eraser print, 92

Fabric design, batik influence, 42
Fabrics
  caring for decorated, 175-178
  ironing temperatures for (table), 178
  for silk screen, 107
Fast-drying pigments, 140
Fillers, removing from cloth, 24
Flock and flocking, 2, 155
Foot pressure, in block printing, 73
Frame
  for batik, 44
  for silk screen, 107
Freeform design, developing, 17
Freehand painting, 2, 94-101
Freehand work, in silk screen, 128
Full-drop repeat, 26
Full repeat, 26

Glitter, 152

Half-drop repeat, 26

Hands, caring for, 144
Heat-setting, 15, 39, 79, 80
  with infra-red lamp, 88
Homemade pigments, 141
Homemade relief paints, 152

Indigo, 168
Infra-red lamp, for heat-setting, 88
Ink
  applying to block, 79
  use for batik, 45
  for block printing, 71
  removing unwanted from blocks, 87
Inverting repeat pattern, 27
Iron oxide, 169
Ironing
  decorated fabrics, 177
  temperature settings for (table, 178

Jig, for registering blocks, 84

Kermes, 169
Kits
  ballpoint, 154
  for block printing, 81
  for flocking, 157
  for relief painting, 151
  silk screen, 110
Knives, for stencil cutting, 11

Lacquer film, for silk screen, 116
Lacquer film stencil, removing, 125
Lacquer-base pigments, 140
Laying out
  of repeat pattern, 37
  for silk screen, 133
Layout
  for batik, 46
  planning, 30, 31
Light value, 162
Linoleum
  cutting techniques, 76, 77
  mounting, 78
  types, 71
Linoleum block, cleaning, 80
Linoleum block printing, 67-88
Logwood, 168

Mallet, in block printing, 72
Materials, sources of, 179
Metallic bronzing powders, 152
Mineral dyes, 169
Mordants, 12, 62, 95, 140
  history, 167
  in modern dyes, 169
Multicolor block printing, 82-88

Natural forms, as printing surface,
  93
Naturalistic form, in design, 17
Non-curing pigments, 141
Novelty decorations, 2, 146-160

Oil base pigments, 140
Oil can, use for tjanting, 45
Orseille, 168
Outline printing (block), 75
Oven, using for heat-setting, 39
Over-all repeat, planning, 25-32
Over-dyeing, 46, 170

Paint
  for block printing, 91
  for freehand work, 94
Paper stencil, for silk screen, 110
Patterns, perforated, 148
Phosphorescent pigments, 141
Pictures, transferring to cloth, 159
Pigments
  for silk screen, 139
  universal, 158
Positive printing (block), 75
Potato print, 91
Potato masher print, 93
Pouncing powder, 49, 148, 154
Pressing, decorated fabrics, 177
Pressure adhesive tape, to form
  printing design, 114
Primary colors, 161
Printing board, 21, 36, 86
  in block printing, 81

Register
  cutting stencils in, 33
  need for, 127
  in two-color work, 83
Register device

for cutting blocks, 84
on printing board, 87
in silk screen, 136
Register marks, block printing, 79
Reinforcements, loose-leaf, in silk
  screen design, 114
Relief painting, 146
Relief paints, 152
Repeat, planning over-all, 25-32
Repeat patterns
  in freehand work, 97
  planning, 80
  silk screening, 116-127
  techniques for variety, 27
  in tie dyeing, 60
  two-color, 33-40
  types of, 26
Resist dyeing, 41
Resist technique, 8
Reverse printing (block), 75
Reverse spatter technique, 98
Reversing repeat pattern, 27
Rinsing, dyed fabric, 172
Rolling pin, in block printing, 72
Rosette, in tie dyeing, 60
Rotating repeat pattern, 27
Rubber bands, as printing surface,
  92
Rubber gloves, 62
  in dyeing, 43
Rubber stamps, 70

Saffron, 168
Salt, see Mordant, 170
Sampler, of tie dye techniques, 66
Samples
  of dyeing results, 173
  gallery of, 180-193
Screening, see Silk screen
Secondary colors, 161
  mixing, 162
Sequinettes, 152
Shades, 163
  mixing, 163
  producing in dye bath, 172
Shellac, use in silk screen, 109
Shellac stencil, for silk screen, 112
Shellfish, 169
Silk, attaching to frame, 108

Silk screen printing, 2, 7, 102-138
  basic technique, 102
  cleanliness in, 142
  lacquer film method, 116
  paper stencil method, 110
  pigments for, 139
  preserving lacquer film stencil,
    124
  shellac stencil method, 112
  solvents (table), 144
  tusche-glue method, 128
  wiping technique for, 143
Silk screening, adhesive for block,
  157
Solvents
  in silk screen, 143
  in silk screen, (table), 144
  for stenciling ink, 13
  in tusche-glue method, 130
Spangles, 152
Spatter techniques, 97
Spoon, in block printing, 73
Spot design techniques, 146
Spray gun, for flocking, 156
Squeegee, 107
Stains and spots, removing from
  decorated fabrics, 173, 176
Starch, removing from cloth, 24
Stencil
  cleaning, 15
  cutting, 13
  cutting in register, 34
Stenciling, 1, 8-24
  adhesive for flock, 157
  border repeat, 20-24
  cleaning up after, 19
  first color, 38
  planning locations of prints, 18
  silk screen as, 102
  technique of, 15
Stencil board, 11
Stone block, 3
Supplies, sources of, 179

Tape, in making silk screen, 109
Tertiary colors, 164
Textile decoration
  defined, 1
  history, 2

Textile paints, 140
Texture, creating in silk screen, 136
Thread, for tie dyeing, 60
Tie dyeing, 2, 5, 58-66
  planning design for, 63
Ties
  in design, 6, 9
  designing, 10
Tints
  of color, 162
  in dyeing, 62
  mixing, 163
  producing in dye bath, 172
Tjanting tool, 45
Tools, for cutting linoleum blocks,
  71
Tusche-glue method, 128
  and Batik, 42
  variations of, 135
Two-color printing, types of register, 83

Umbrella rib, as cutting tool, 72
Universal pigments, 158

Varigated pattern, in tie dyeing, 65
Vegetable dyes, 168
Vessel, for dyeing, 60, 170
Vinegar, *see* Mordant, 170

Washer, dyeing in, 173
Washing, decorated fabrics, 175
Water base pigments, 140
White space, in designing, 29
Wax
  molten, 4
  preparing batik, 44
  removing from cloth, 51
Wiping technique in cleaning screen,
  143
Wood block, 2, 89, 90
  carved, 70
  for mounting linoleum, 68, 71, 72
  in tie dyeing, 65
Wood grain, in prints, 90
Wringing decorated fabrics, 176

Yard stick, as guide line, 24

A CATALOG OF SELECTED
DOVER BOOKS
IN ALL FIELDS OF INTEREST

DRAWINGS OF REMBRANDT, edited by Seymour Slive. Updated Lippmann, Hofstede de Groot edition, with definitive scholarly apparatus. All portraits, biblical sketches, landscapes, nudes. Oriental figures, classical studies, together with selection of work by followers. 550 illustrations. Total of 630pp. 9⅛ × 12¼.
21485-0, 21486-9 Pa., Two-vol. set $29.90

GHOST AND HORROR STORIES OF AMBROSE BIERCE, Ambrose Bierce. 24 tales vividly imagined, strangely prophetic, and decades ahead of their time in technical skill: "The Damned Thing," "An Inhabitant of Carcosa," "The Eyes of the Panther," "Moxon's Master," and 20 more. 199pp. 5⅜ × 8½.   20767-6 Pa. $4.95

ETHICAL WRITINGS OF MAIMONIDES, Maimonides. Most significant ethical works of great medieval sage, newly translated for utmost precision, readability. Laws Concerning Character Traits, Eight Chapters, more. 192pp. 5⅜ × 8½.
24522-5 Pa. $4.50

THE EXPLORATION OF THE COLORADO RIVER AND ITS CANYONS, J. W. Powell. Full text of Powell's 1,000-mile expedition down the fabled Colorado in 1869. Superb account of terrain, geology, vegetation, Indians, famine, mutiny, treacherous rapids, mighty canyons, during exploration of last unknown part of continental U.S. 400pp. 5⅜ × 8½.   20094-9 Pa. $7.95

HISTORY OF PHILOSOPHY, Julián Marías. Clearest one-volume history on the market. Every major philosopher and dozens of others, to Existentialism and later. 505pp. 5⅜ × 8½.   21739-6 Pa. $9.95

ALL ABOUT LIGHTNING, Martin A. Uman. Highly readable nontechnical survey of nature and causes of lightning, thunderstorms, ball lightning, St. Elmo's Fire, much more. Illustrated. 192pp. 5⅜ × 8½.   25237-X Pa. $5.95

SAILING ALONE AROUND THE WORLD, Captain Joshua Slocum. First man to sail around the world, alone, in small boat. One of great feats of seamanship told in delightful manner. 67 illustrations. 294pp. 5⅜ × 8½.   20326-3 Pa. $4.95

LETTERS AND NOTES ON THE MANNERS, CUSTOMS AND CONDITIONS OF THE NORTH AMERICAN INDIANS, George Catlin. Classic account of life among Plains Indians: ceremonies, hunt, warfare, etc. 312 plates. 572pp. of text. 6⅛ × 9¼.   22118-0, 22119-9, Pa., Two-vol. set $17.90

ALASKA: The Harriman Expedition, 1899, John Burroughs, John Muir, et al. Informative, engrossing accounts of two-month, 9,000-mile expedition. Native peoples, wildlife, forests, geography, salmon industry, glaciers, more. Profusely illustrated. 240 black-and-white line drawings. 124 black-and-white photographs. 3 maps. Index. 576pp. 5⅜ × 8½.   25109-8 Pa. $11.95

THE ART NOUVEAU STYLE BOOK OF ALPHONSE MUCHA: All 72 Plates from "Documents Decoratifs" in Original Color, Alphonse Mucha. Rare copyright-free design portfolio by high priest of Art Nouveau. Jewelry, wallpaper, stained glass, furniture, figure studies, plant and animal motifs, etc. Only complete one-volume edition. 80pp. 9⅜ × 12¼. 24044-4 Pa. $10.95

ANIMALS: 1,419 Copyright-Free Illustrations of Mammals, Birds, Fish, Insects, Etc., edited by Jim Harter. Clear wood engravings present, in extremely lifelike poses, over 1,000 species of animals. One of the most extensive pictorial source-books of its kind. Captions. Index. 284pp. 9 × 12. 23766-4 Pa. $10.95

OBELISTS FLY HIGH, C. Daly King. Masterpiece of American detective fiction, long out of print, involves murder on a 1935 transcontinental flight—"a very thrilling story"—NY Times. Unabridged and unaltered republication of the edition published by William Collins Sons & Co. Ltd., London, 1935. 288pp. 5⅜ × 8½. (Available in U.S. only) 25036-9 Pa. $5.95

VICTORIAN AND EDWARDIAN FASHION: A Photographic Survey, Alison Gernsheim. First fashion history completely illustrated by contemporary photographs. Full text plus 235 photos, 1840–1914, in which many celebrities appear. 240pp. 6½ × 9¼. 24205-6 Pa. $8.95

THE ART OF THE FRENCH ILLUSTRATED BOOK, 1700–1914, Gordon N. Ray. Over 630 superb book illustrations by Fragonard, Delacroix, Daumier, Doré, Grandville, Manet, Mucha, Steinlen, Toulouse-Lautrec and many others. Preface. Introduction. 633 halftones. Indices of artists, authors & titles, binders and provenances. Appendices. Bibliography. 608pp. 8⅜ × 11¼. 25086-5 Pa. $24.95

THE WONDERFUL WIZARD OF OZ, L. Frank Baum. Facsimile in full color of America's finest children's classic. 143 illustrations by W. W. Denslow. 267pp. 5⅜ × 8½. 20691-2 Pa. $7.95

FOLLOWING THE EQUATOR: A Journey Around the World, Mark Twain. Great writer's 1897 account of circumnavigating the globe by steamship. Ironic humor, keen observations, vivid and fascinating descriptions of exotic places. 197 illustrations. 720pp. 5⅜ × 8½. 26113-1 Pa. $15.95

THE FRIENDLY STARS, Martha Evans Martin & Donald Howard Menzel. Classic text marshalls the stars together in an engaging, nontechnical survey, presenting them as sources of beauty in night sky. 23 illustrations. Foreword. 2 star charts. Index. 147pp. 5⅜ × 8½. 21099-5 Pa. $3.95

FADS AND FALLACIES IN THE NAME OF SCIENCE, Martin Gardner. Fair, witty appraisal of cranks, quacks, and quackeries of science and pseudoscience: hollow earth, Velikovsky, orgone energy, Dianetics, flying saucers, Bridey Murphy, food and medical fads, etc. Revised, expanded In the Name of Science. "A very able and even-tempered presentation."—The New Yorker. 363pp. 5⅜ × 8. 20394-8 Pa. $6.95

ANCIENT EGYPT: Its Culture and History, J. E. Manchip White. From pre-dynastics through Ptolemies: society, history, political structure, religion, daily life, literature, cultural heritage. 48 plates. 217pp. 5⅜ × 8½. 22548-8 Pa. $5.95

SUNDIALS, Albert Waugh. Far and away the best, most thorough coverage of ideas, mathematics concerned, types, construction, adjusting anywhere. Over 100 illustrations. 230pp. 5⅜ × 8½. 22947-5 Pa. $5.95

PICTURE HISTORY OF THE NORMANDIE: With 190 Illustrations, Frank O. Braynard. Full story of legendary French ocean liner: Art Deco interiors, design innovations, furnishings, celebrities, maiden voyage, tragic fire, much more. Extensive text. 144pp. 8⅞ × 11¾. 25257-4 Pa. $10.95

THE FIRST AMERICAN COOKBOOK: A Facsimile of "American Cookery," 1796, Amelia Simmons. Facsimile of the first American-written cookbook published in the United States contains authentic recipes for colonial favorites—pumpkin pudding, winter squash pudding, spruce beer, Indian slapjacks, and more. Introductory Essay and Glossary of colonial cooking terms. 80pp. 5⅜ × 8½. 24710-4 Pa. $3.50

101 PUZZLES IN THOUGHT AND LOGIC, C. R. Wylie, Jr. Solve murders and robberies, find out which fishermen are liars, how a blind man could possibly identify a color—purely by your own reasoning! 107pp. 5⅜ × 8½. 20367-0 Pa. $2.95

ANCIENT EGYPTIAN MYTHS AND LEGENDS, Lewis Spence. Examines animism, totemism, fetishism, creation myths, deities, alchemy, art and magic, other topics. Over 50 illustrations. 432pp. 5⅜ × 8½. 26525-0 Pa. $8.95

ANTHROPOLOGY AND MODERN LIFE, Franz Boas. Great anthropologist's classic treatise on race and culture. Introduction by Ruth Bunzel. Only inexpensive paperback edition. 255pp. 5⅜ × 8½. 25245-0 Pa. $6.95

THE TALE OF PETER RABBIT, Beatrix Potter. The inimitable Peter's terrifying adventure in Mr. McGregor's garden, with all 27 wonderful, full-color Potter illustrations. 55pp. 4¼ × 5½. (Available in U.S. only) 22827-4 Pa. $1.75

THREE PROPHETIC SCIENCE FICTION NOVELS, H. G. Wells. *When the Sleeper Wakes, A Story of the Days to Come* and *The Time Machine* (full version). 335pp. 5⅜ × 8½. (Available in U.S. only) 20605-X Pa. $8.95

APICIUS COOKERY AND DINING IN IMPERIAL ROME, edited and translated by Joseph Dommers Vehling. Oldest known cookbook in existence offers readers a clear picture of what foods Romans ate, how they prepared them, etc. 49 illustrations. 301pp. 6⅛ × 9¼. 23563-7 Pa. $7.95

SHAKESPEARE LEXICON AND QUOTATION DICTIONARY, Alexander Schmidt. Full definitions, locations, shades of meaning of every word in plays and poems. More than 50,000 exact quotations. 1,485pp. 6½ × 9¼. 22726-X, 22727-8 Pa., Two-vol. set $31.90

THE WORLD'S GREAT SPEECHES, edited by Lewis Copeland and Lawrence W. Lamm. Vast collection of 278 speeches from Greeks to 1970. Powerful and effective models; unique look at history. 842pp. 5⅜ × 8½. 20468-5 Pa. $12.95

ILLUSTRATED GUIDE TO SHAKER FURNITURE, Robert Meader. All furniture and appurtenances, with much on unknown local styles. 235 photos. 146pp. 9 × 12.   22819-3 Pa. $8.95

WHALE SHIPS AND WHALING: A Pictorial Survey, George Francis Dow. Over 200 vintage engravings, drawings, photographs of barks, brigs, cutters, other vessels. Also harpoons, lances, whaling guns, many other artifacts. Comprehensive text by foremost authority. 207 black-and-white illustrations. 288pp. 6 × 9.
24808-9 Pa. $9.95

THE BERTRAMS, Anthony Trollope. Powerful portrayal of blind self-will and thwarted ambition includes one of Trollope's most heartrending love stories. 497pp. 5⅜ × 8½.   25119-5 Pa. $9.95

ADVENTURES WITH A HAND LENS, Richard Headstrom. Clearly written guide to observing and studying flowers and grasses, fish scales, moth and insect wings, egg cases, buds, feathers, seeds, leaf scars, moss, molds, ferns, common crystals, etc.—all with an ordinary, inexpensive magnifying glass. 209 exact line drawings aid in your discoveries. 220pp. 5⅜ × 8½.   23330-8 Pa. $5.95

RODIN ON ART AND ARTISTS, Auguste Rodin. Great sculptor's candid, wide-ranging comments on meaning of art; great artists; relation of sculpture to poetry, painting, music; philosophy of life, more. 76 superb black-and-white illustrations of Rodin's sculpture, drawings and prints. 119pp. 8⅜ × 11¼.   24487-3 Pa. $7.95

FIFTY CLASSIC FRENCH FILMS, 1912–1982: A Pictorial Record, Anthony Slide. Memorable stills from Grand Illusion, Beauty and the Beast, Hiroshima, Mon Amour, many more. Credits, plot synopses, reviews, etc. 160pp. 8¼ × 11.
25256-6 Pa. $11.95

THE PRINCIPLES OF PSYCHOLOGY, William James. Famous long course complete, unabridged. Stream of thought, time perception, memory, experimental methods; great work decades ahead of its time. 94 figures. 1,391pp. 5⅜ × 8½.
20381-6, 20382-4 Pa., Two-vol. set $25.90

BODIES IN A BOOKSHOP, R. T. Campbell. Challenging mystery of blackmail and murder with ingenious plot and superbly drawn characters. In the best tradition of British suspense fiction. 192pp. 5⅜ × 8½.   24720-1 Pa. $4.95

CALLAS: Portrait of a Prima Donna, George Jellinek. Renowned commentator on the musical scene chronicles incredible career and life of the most controversial, fascinating, influential operatic personality of our time. 64 black-and-white photographs. 416pp. 5⅜ × 8¼.   25047-4 Pa. $8.95

GEOMETRY, RELATIVITY AND THE FOURTH DIMENSION, Rudolph Rucker. Exposition of fourth dimension, concepts of relativity as Flatland characters continue adventures. Popular, easily followed yet accurate, profound. 141 illustrations. 133pp. 5⅜ × 8½.   23400-2 Pa. $4.95

HOUSEHOLD STORIES BY THE BROTHERS GRIMM, with pictures by Walter Crane. 53 classic stories—Rumpelstiltskin, Rapunzel, Hansel and Gretel, the Fisherman and his Wife, Snow White, Tom Thumb, Sleeping Beauty, Cinderella, and so much more—lavishly illustrated with original 19th-century drawings. 114 illustrations. x + 269pp. 5⅜ × 8½.   21080-4 Pa. $4.95

CHRISTMAS CUSTOMS AND TRADITIONS, Clement A. Miles. Origin, evolution, significance of religious, secular practices. Caroling, gifts, yule logs, much more. Full, scholarly yet fascinating; non-sectarian. 400pp. 5⅜ × 8½.
23354-5 Pa. $6.95

THE HUMAN FIGURE IN MOTION, Eadweard Muybridge. More than 4,500 stopped-action photos, in action series, showing undraped men, women, children jumping, lying down, throwing, sitting, wrestling, carrying, etc. 390pp. 7⅞ × 10⅝.
20204-6 Cloth. $24.95

THE MAN WHO WAS THURSDAY, Gilbert Keith Chesterton. Witty, fast-paced novel about a club of anarchists in turn-of-the-century London. Brilliant social, religious, philosophical speculations. 128pp. 5⅜ × 8½.
25121-7 Pa. $3.95

A CÉZANNE SKETCHBOOK: Figures, Portraits, Landscapes and Still Lifes, Paul Cézanne. Great artist experiments with tonal effects, light, mass, other qualities in over 100 drawings. A revealing view of developing master painter, precursor of Cubism. 102 black-and-white illustrations. 144pp. 8¾ × 6⅜.
24790-2 Pa. $6.95

AN ENCYCLOPEDIA OF BATTLES: Accounts of Over 1,560 Battles from 1479 B.C. to the Present, David Eggenberger. Presents essential details of every major battle in recorded history, from the first battle of Megiddo in 1479 B.C. to Grenada in 1984. List of Battle Maps. New Appendix covering the years 1967–1984. Index. 99 illustrations. 544pp. 6½ × 9¼.
24913-1 Pa. $14.95

AN ETYMOLOGICAL DICTIONARY OF MODERN ENGLISH, Ernest Weekley. Richest, fullest work, by foremost British lexicographer. Detailed word histories. Inexhaustible. Total of 856pp. 6½ × 9¼.
21873-2, 21874-0 Pa., Two-vol. set $19.90

WEBSTER'S AMERICAN MILITARY BIOGRAPHIES, edited by Robert McHenry. Over 1,000 figures who shaped 3 centuries of American military history. Detailed biographies of Nathan Hale, Douglas MacArthur, Mary Hallaren, others. Chronologies of engagements, more. Introduction. Addenda. 1,033 entries in alphabetical order. xi + 548pp. 6½ × 9¼. (Available in U.S. only)
24758-9 Pa. $13.95

LIFE IN ANCIENT EGYPT, Adolf Erman. Detailed older account, with much not in more recent books: domestic life, religion, magic, medicine, commerce, and whatever else needed for complete picture. Many illustrations. 597pp. 5⅜ × 8½.
22632-8 Pa. $8.95

HISTORIC COSTUME IN PICTURES, Braun & Schneider. Over 1,450 costumed figures shown, covering a wide variety of peoples: kings, emperors, nobles, priests, servants, soldiers, scholars, townsfolk, peasants, merchants, courtiers, cavaliers, and more. 256pp. 8⅜ × 11¼.
23150-X Pa. $9.95

THE NOTEBOOKS OF LEONARDO DA VINCI, edited by J. P. Richter. Extracts from manuscripts reveal great genius; on painting, sculpture, anatomy, sciences, geography, etc. Both Italian and English. 186 ms. pages reproduced, plus 500 additional drawings, including studies for Last Supper, Sforza monument, etc. 860pp. 7⅞ × 10¾. (Available in U.S. only) 22572-0, 22573-9 Pa., Two-vol. set $31.90

A CONCISE HISTORY OF PHOTOGRAPHY: Third Revised Edition, Helmut Gernsheim. Best one-volume history—camera obscura, photochemistry, daguerreotypes, evolution of cameras, film, more. Also artistic aspects—landscape, portraits, fine art, etc. 281 black-and-white photographs. 26 in color. 176pp. 8⅜ × 11¼.
25128-4 Pa. $14.95

THE DORÉ BIBLE ILLUSTRATIONS, Gustave Doré. 241 detailed plates from the Bible: the Creation scenes, Adam and Eve, Flood, Babylon, battle sequences, life of Jesus, etc. Each plate is accompanied by the verses from the King James version of the Bible. 241pp. 9 × 12. 23004-X Pa. $9.95

WANDERINGS IN WEST AFRICA, Richard F. Burton. Great Victorian scholar/adventurer's invaluable descriptions of African tribal rituals, fetishism, culture, art, much more. Fascinating 19th-century account. 624pp. 5⅜ × 8½. 26890-X Pa. $12.95

FLATLAND, E. A. Abbott. Intriguing and enormously popular science-fiction classic explores the complexities of trying to survive as a two-dimensional being in a three-dimensional world. Amusingly illustrated by the author. 16 illustrations. 103pp. 5⅜ × 8½. 20001-9 Pa. $2.50

THE HISTORY OF THE LEWIS AND CLARK EXPEDITION, Meriwether Lewis and William Clark, edited by Elliott Coues. Classic edition of Lewis and Clark's day-by-day journals that later became the basis for U.S. claims to Oregon and the West. Accurate and invaluable geographical, botanical, biological, meteorological and anthropological material. Total of 1,508pp. 5⅜ × 8½.
21268-8, 21269-6, 21270-X Pa., Three-vol. set $29.85

LANGUAGE, TRUTH AND LOGIC, Alfred J. Ayer. Famous, clear introduction to Vienna, Cambridge schools of Logical Positivism. Role of philosophy, elimination of metaphysics, nature of analysis, etc. 160pp. 5⅜ × 8½. (Available in U.S. and Canada only) 20010-8 Pa. $3.95

MATHEMATICS FOR THE NONMATHEMATICIAN, Morris Kline. Detailed, college-level treatment of mathematics in cultural and historical context, with numerous exercises. For liberal arts students. Preface. Recommended Reading Lists. Tables. Index. Numerous black-and-white figures. xvi + 641pp. 5⅜ × 8½.
24823-2 Pa. $11.95

HANDBOOK OF PICTORIAL SYMBOLS, Rudolph Modley. 3,250 signs and symbols, many systems in full; official or heavy commercial use. Arranged by subject. Most in Pictorial Archive series. 143pp. 8⅜ × 11. 23357-X Pa. $7.95

INCIDENTS OF TRAVEL IN YUCATAN, John L. Stephens. Classic (1843) exploration of jungles of Yucatan, looking for evidences of Maya civilization. Travel adventures, Mexican and Indian culture, etc. Total of 669pp. 5⅜ × 8½.
20926-1, 20927-X Pa., Two-vol. set $11.90

THE BLUE FAIRY BOOK, Andrew Lang. The first, most famous collection, with many familiar tales: Little Red Riding Hood, Aladdin and the Wonderful Lamp, Puss in Boots, Sleeping Beauty, Hansel and Gretel, Rumpelstiltskin; 37 in all. 138 illustrations. 390pp. 5⅜ × 8½. 21437-0 Pa. $6.95

THE STORY OF THE CHAMPIONS OF THE ROUND TABLE, Howard Pyle. Sir Launcelot, Sir Tristram and Sir Percival in spirited adventures of love and triumph retold in Pyle's inimitable style. 50 drawings, 31 full-page. xviii + 329pp. 6½ × 9¼. 21883-X Pa. $7.95

THE MYTHS OF THE NORTH AMERICAN INDIANS, Lewis Spence. Myths and legends of the Algonquins, Iroquois, Pawnees and Sioux with comprehensive historical and ethnological commentary. 36 illustrations. 5⅜ × 8½. 25967-6 Pa. $8.95

GREAT DINOSAUR HUNTERS AND THEIR DISCOVERIES, Edwin H. Colbert. Fascinating, lavishly illustrated chronicle of dinosaur research, 1820s to 1960. Achievements of Cope, Marsh, Brown, Buckland, Mantell, Huxley, many others. 384pp. 5¼ × 8¼. 24701-5 Pa. $7.95

THE TASTEMAKERS, Russell Lynes. Informal, illustrated social history of American taste 1850s-1950s. First popularized categories Highbrow, Lowbrow, Middlebrow. 129 illustrations. New (1979) afterword. 384pp. 6 × 9. 23993-4 Pa. $8.95

DOUBLE CROSS PURPOSES, Ronald A. Knox. A treasure hunt in the Scottish Highlands, an old map, unidentified corpse, surprise discoveries keep reader guessing in this cleverly intricate tale of financial skullduggery. 2 black-and-white maps. 320pp. 5⅜ × 8½. (Available in U.S. only) 25032-6 Pa. $6.95

AUTHENTIC VICTORIAN DECORATION AND ORNAMENTATION IN FULL COLOR: 46 Plates from "Studies in Design," Christopher Dresser. Superb full-color lithographs reproduced from rare original portfolio of a major Victorian designer. 48pp. 9¼ × 12¼. 25083-0 Pa. $7.95

PRIMITIVE ART, Franz Boas. Remains the best text ever prepared on subject, thoroughly discussing Indian, African, Asian, Australian, and, especially, Northern American primitive art. Over 950 illustrations show ceramics, masks, totem poles, weapons, textiles, paintings, much more. 376pp. 5⅜ × 8. 20025-6 Pa. $7.95

SIDELIGHTS ON RELATIVITY, Albert Einstein. Unabridged republication of two lectures delivered by the great physicist in 1920–21. *Ether and Relativity* and *Geometry and Experience.* Elegant ideas in nonmathematical form, accessible to intelligent layman. vi + 56pp. 5⅜ × 8½. 24511-X Pa. $3.95

THE WIT AND HUMOR OF OSCAR WILDE, edited by Alvin Redman. More than 1,000 ripostes, paradoxes, wisecracks: Work is the curse of the drinking classes, I can resist everything except temptation, etc. 258pp. 5⅜ × 8½. 20602-5 Pa. $4.95

ADVENTURES WITH A MICROSCOPE, Richard Headstrom. 59 adventures with clothing fibers, protozoa, ferns and lichens, roots and leaves, much more. 142 illustrations. 232pp. 5⅜ × 8½. 23471-1 Pa. $3.95

PLANTS OF THE BIBLE, Harold N. Moldenke and Alma L. Moldenke. Standard reference to all 230 plants mentioned in Scriptures. Latin name, biblical reference, uses, modern identity, much more. Unsurpassed encyclopedic resource for scholars, botanists, nature lovers, students of Bible. Bibliography. Indexes. 123 black-and-white illustrations. 384pp. 6 × 9. 25069-5 Pa. $8.95

FAMOUS AMERICAN WOMEN: A Biographical Dictionary from Colonial Times to the Present, Robert McHenry, ed. From Pocahontas to Rosa Parks, 1,035 distinguished American women documented in separate biographical entries. Accurate, up-to-date data, numerous categories, spans 400 years. Indices. 493pp. 6½ × 9¼. 24523-3 Pa. $10.95

THE FABULOUS INTERIORS OF THE GREAT OCEAN LINERS IN HISTORIC PHOTOGRAPHS, William H. Miller, Jr. Some 200 superb photographs capture exquisite interiors of world's great "floating palaces"—1890s to 1980s: *Titanic, Ile de France, Queen Elizabeth, United States, Europa,* more. Approx. 200 black-and-white photographs. Captions. Text. Introduction. 160pp. 8⅞ × 11¾. 24756-2 Pa. $9.95

THE GREAT LUXURY LINERS, 1927–1954: A Photographic Record, William H. Miller, Jr. Nostalgic tribute to heyday of ocean liners. 186 photos of *Ile de France, Normandie, Leviathan, Queen Elizabeth, United States,* many others. Interior and exterior views. Introduction. Captions. 160pp. 9 × 12. 24056-8 Pa. $10.95

A NATURAL HISTORY OF THE DUCKS, John Charles Phillips. Great landmark of ornithology offers complete detailed coverage of nearly 200 species and subspecies of ducks: gadwall, sheldrake, merganser, pintail, many more. 74 full-color plates, 102 black-and-white. Bibliography. Total of 1,920pp. 8⅝ × 11¼. 25141-1, 25142-X Cloth., Two-vol. set $100.00

THE SEAWEED HANDBOOK: An Illustrated Guide to Seaweeds from North Carolina to Canada, Thomas F. Lee. Concise reference covers 78 species. Scientific and common names, habitat, distribution, more. Finding keys for easy identification. 224pp. 5⅜ × 8½. 25215-9 Pa. $6.95

THE TEN BOOKS OF ARCHITECTURE: The 1755 Leoni Edition, Leon Battista Alberti. Rare classic helped introduce the glories of ancient architecture to the Renaissance. 68 black-and-white plates. 336pp. 8⅜ × 11¼. 25239-6 Pa. $14.95

MISS MACKENZIE, Anthony Trollope. Minor masterpieces by Victorian master unmasks many truths about life in 19th-century England. First inexpensive edition in years. 392pp. 5⅜ × 8½. 25201-9 Pa. $8.95

THE RIME OF THE ANCIENT MARINER, Gustave Doré, Samuel Taylor Coleridge. Dramatic engravings considered by many to be his greatest work. The terrifying space of the open sea, the storms and whirlpools of an unknown ocean, the ice of Antarctica, more—all rendered in a powerful, chilling manner. Full text. 38 plates. 77pp. 9¼ × 12. 22305-1 Pa. $4.95

THE EXPEDITIONS OF ZEBULON MONTGOMERY PIKE, Zebulon Montgomery Pike. Fascinating firsthand accounts (1805–6) of exploration of Mississippi River, Indian wars, capture by Spanish dragoons, much more. 1,088pp. 5⅜ × 8½. 25254-X, 25255-8 Pa., Two-vol. set $25.90

DEGAS: An Intimate Portrait, Ambroise Vollard. Charming, anecdotal memoir by famous art dealer of one of the greatest 19th-century French painters. 14 black-and-white illustrations. Introduction by Harold L. Van Doren. 96pp. 5⅜ × 8½.
25131-4 Pa. $4.95

PERSONAL NARRATIVE OF A PILGRIMAGE TO AL-MADINAH AND MECCAH, Richard F. Burton. Great travel classic by remarkably colorful personality. Burton, disguised as a Moroccan, visited sacred shrines of Islam, narrowly escaping death. 47 illustrations. 959pp. 5⅜ × 8½.
21217-3, 21218-1 Pa., Two-vol. set $19.90

PHRASE AND WORD ORIGINS, A. H. Holt. Entertaining, reliable, modern study of more than 1,200 colorful words, phrases, origins and histories. Much unexpected information. 254pp. 5⅜ × 8½. 20758-7 Pa. $5.95

THE RED THUMB MARK, R. Austin Freeman. In this first Dr. Thorndyke case, the great scientific detective draws fascinating conclusions from the nature of a single fingerprint. Exciting story, authentic science. 320pp. 5⅜ × 8½. (Available in U.S. only) 25210-8 Pa. $6.95

AN EGYPTIAN HIEROGLYPHIC DICTIONARY, E. A. Wallis Budge. Monumental work containing about 25,000 words or terms that occur in texts ranging from 3000 B.C. to 600 A.D. Each entry consists of a transliteration of the word, the word in hieroglyphs, and the meaning in English. 1,314pp. 6⅝ × 10.
23615-3, 23616-1 Pa., Two-vol. set $35.90

THE COMPLEAT STRATEGYST: Being a Primer on the Theory of Games of Strategy, J. D. Williams. Highly entertaining classic describes, with many illustrated examples, how to select best strategies in conflict situations. Prefaces. Appendices. xvi + 268pp. 5⅜ × 8½. 25101-2 Pa. $6.95

THE ROAD TO OZ, L. Frank Baum. Dorothy meets the Shaggy Man, little Button-Bright and the Rainbow's beautiful daughter in this delightful trip to the magical Land of Oz. 272pp. 5⅜ × 8. 25208-6 Pa. $5.95

POINT AND LINE TO PLANE, Wassily Kandinsky. Seminal exposition of role of point, line, other elements in nonobjective painting. Essential to understanding 20th-century art. 127 illustrations. 192pp. 6½ × 9¼. 23808-3 Pa. $5.95

LADY ANNA, Anthony Trollope. Moving chronicle of Countess Lovel's bitter struggle to win for herself and daughter Anna their rightful rank and fortune—perhaps at cost of sanity itself. 384pp. 5⅜ × 8½. 24669-8 Pa. $8.95

EGYPTIAN MAGIC, E. A. Wallis Budge. Sums up all that is known about magic in Ancient Egypt: the role of magic in controlling the gods, powerful amulets that warded off evil spirits, scarabs of immortality, use of wax images, formulas and spells, the secret name, much more. 253pp. 5⅜ × 8½. 22681-6 Pa. $4.50

THE DANCE OF SIVA, Ananda Coomaraswamy. Preeminent authority unfolds the vast metaphysic of India: the revelation of her art, conception of the universe, social organization, etc. 27 reproductions of art masterpieces. 192pp. 5⅜ × 8½.
24817-8 Pa. $6.95

CATALOG OF DOVER BOOKS

AMERICAN CLIPPER SHIPS: 1833–1858, Octavius T. Howe & Frederick C. Matthews. Fully-illustrated, encyclopedic review of 352 clipper ships from the period of America's greatest maritime supremacy. Introduction. 109 halftones. 5 black-and-white line illustrations. Index. Total of 928pp. 5⅜ × 8½.
25115-2, 25116-0 Pa., Two-vol. set $17.90

TOWARDS A NEW ARCHITECTURE, Le Corbusier. Pioneering manifesto by great architect, near legendary founder of "International School." Technical and aesthetic theories, views on industry, economics, relation of form to function, "mass-production spirit," much more. Profusely illustrated. Unabridged translation of 13th French edition. Introduction by Frederick Etchells. 320pp. 6⅛ × 9¼. (Available in U.S. only) 25023-7 Pa. $8.95

THE BOOK OF KELLS, edited by Blanche Cirker. Inexpensive collection of 32 full-color, full-page plates from the greatest illuminated manuscript of the Middle Ages, painstakingly reproduced from rare facsimile edition. Publisher's Note. Captions. 32pp. 9⅜ × 12¼. 24345-1 Pa. $5.95

BEST SCIENCE FICTION STORIES OF H. G. WELLS, H. G. Wells. Full novel *The Invisible Man,* plus 17 short stories: "The Crystal Egg," "Aepyornis Island," "The Strange Orchid," etc. 303pp. 5⅜ × 8½. (Available in U.S. only)
21531-8 Pa. $6.95

AMERICAN SAILING SHIPS: Their Plans and History, Charles G. Davis. Photos, construction details of schooners, frigates, clippers, other sailcraft of 18th to early 20th centuries—plus entertaining discourse on design, rigging, nautical lore, much more. 137 black-and-white illustrations. 240pp. 6⅛ × 9¼.
24658-2 Pa. $6.95

ENTERTAINING MATHEMATICAL PUZZLES, Martin Gardner. Selection of author's favorite conundrums involving arithmetic, money, speed, etc., with lively commentary. Complete solutions. 112pp. 5⅜ × 8½. 25211-6 Pa. $3.50

THE WILL TO BELIEVE, HUMAN IMMORTALITY, William James. Two books bound together. Effect of irrational on logical, and arguments for human immortality. 402pp. 5⅜ × 8½. 20291-7 Pa. $8.95

THE HAUNTED MONASTERY and THE CHINESE MAZE MURDERS, Robert Van Gulik. 2 full novels by Van Gulik continue adventures of Judge Dee and his companions. An evil Taoist monastery, seemingly supernatural events; overgrown topiary maze that hides strange crimes. Set in 7th-century China. 27 illustrations. 328pp. 5⅜ × 8½. 23502-5 Pa. $6.95

CELEBRATED CASES OF JUDGE DEE (DEE GOONG AN), translated by Robert Van Gulik. Authentic 18th-century Chinese detective novel; Dee and associates solve three interlocked cases. Led to Van Gulik's own stories with same characters. Extensive introduction. 9 illustrations. 237pp. 5⅜ × 8½.
23337-5 Pa. $5.95

Prices subject to change without notice.

Available at your book dealer or write for free catalog to Dept. GI, Dover Publications, Inc., 31 East 2nd St., Mineola, N.Y. 11501. Dover publishes more than 175 books each year on science, elementary and advanced mathematics, biology, music, art, literary history, social sciences and other areas.